Golden Shit

THE BIGGEST MISTAKES I MADE STARTING
MY BUSINESS AND WHAT I LEARNED

Golden Shit

MARISSA FINN

outskirts
press

Mom and dad, this one's for you.

And Will. For all my crazy ideas, you call me crazy for not going after them. And because of that, I found myself again.

Contents

Intro

In 2016, my life exploded. I started a fucking business. Now, I know what you're thinking… A little aggressive coming out of the gate. What the hell am I in for here?

Well, I'll tell you what you're in for: an epic party, followed by a raging hangover, followed by a need to reevaluate your whole life, followed by the best damn beach vacation you've ever had, strawberry daiquiri in hand, sand between your toes, ocean waves calming you into a nice long nap in the sun.

You'll find out why I use the "F Bomb" as an identifier for my business in just a minute. Hang tight.

I used to think it wasn't sexy to have a messy story. I used to believe in "perfect." I used to think that others' opinions defined my life. I used to think that working myself to death was the only way to scale. I used to think my stress would dissipate if I could just get one more client. I used to believe that the success in my business defined my self-worth. I used to believe that coffee was the most powerful force in the world.

Well, people, I'm here to call bullshit on everything (except maybe the coffee thing…).

I'm here to share the gory details: the late nights with multiple bottles of wine, the treks to work, almost falling asleep at the wheel, the mornings I rolled out of bed crying from exhaustion, the trips to the coffee shop in the same clothes I wore for five days straight, the weeks of eating only ramen noodles for three meals a day, the adult acne that punched me in the face, and the days I forgot to brush my teeth because I was so engrossed in moving the needle forward, trying to do all of the madness at once and with rancid morning breath.

I walked through a lot of shit, as does everyone on the way to their dreams. But the difference is, I am not trying to cover it up. I don't believe in hiding the mess, but instead, I'm sharing it with those who are walking the path after me, in hopes that they don't trip over the same damn branch or step in the same pile of dog poop.

I used to believe that being emotional was a weakness. I used to believe that being so passionate that your dream overtakes and consumes your life was a bad thing, until I learned how to use that passion, use that emotion to be powerful, impactful. There are a lot of people who are too scared to put it all on the table because society has conditioned us to keep it inside, you know, in case it might bother someone else. But the further along I walked this journey of being an entrepreneur, the more I realized that it is our duty, our superpower, to use our voices to create change for the people who need us, the people who are walking this journey a few steps behind us.

You see, for the longest time I tried so hard to cover up my mistakes instead of using them to move the needle forward, learn from them, and move on. I spent so much time in denial that they either weren't happening or that I would come out of them with zero effort, nail polish still intact. HOWEVER, I soon came to realize that pretty "reality" was simply a delusion.

What no one tells you is that the hardest part is not the initial jump toward your dream, but going through the shit and then *getting out of* the shit on your way up the mountain. The hardest part is waking up day after day when your life is a hot mess, continuing to move forward, one foot in front of the other, trudging through a Minnesota blizzard to get to the pretty part of chasing your dream on the other side. Now, I won't focus on the pretty part because that part is already covered in ALL the self-help/business owner wannabe books out there. Because the pretty part is the fun part. That's the part that won't trigger you to run out into the rain in your underwear.

The life you live is 100 percent yours—not your judgy neighbor's life, who makes you feel incapable because your grass is a little too long; not your friend's life, who makes you feel like dirt that you're working again and not out drinking; and not the guy-next-to-you-at-the-gym's life, who's glaring at you for dancing on the treadmill because Beyoncé came on and it was necessary.

YOURS.

I started this book because I felt compelled to tell my story. I was sick of all the books that sugarcoat what it's *actually* like on the road trip to your dream life, and was waiting to hear one that resonated with my story, what *I* went through in starting my business. And the more books I read, the more I came up short, the more I felt like a failure, because none of them highlighted the truth.

I'm here to tell you the mistakes I made along the way. How I was incapable of sex for almost two years, how I constantly had stress balls (yes, actual BALLS) in my shoulders, how I developed an eating disorder, how I let the shit-talking of others physically stop me from going after my dream life, how an identity crisis caused me to have panic attacks because I believed the story that *other people* had actually made up for me, and so many other things that sent me spiraling over the edge while scaling my business.

YOU GUYS! I am here to set it all straight. I am here to give you love and guidance and a swift kick in the rear to go chase after the things you want most in life. I'm busting down the doors of your limiting beliefs, squirt guns in hand, ready to piss some people off.

Because it is time.

You're going places. And this book is your guiding light. Because this is the golden shit no one tells you—the nasty, stinky, 2:00 a.m. cab ride home. But you know what? That shit is what keeps the journey interesting, what fuels you forward. It's because of the golden shit that you'll look back on your journey to the top and tell yourself how cute it was that you were actually stressing about learning self-care, or how ridiculous it was that you were questioning whether to take the scary jump in the first place. But first an intro, so I'm not just some crazy lady giving it to you straight—at least now you'll know my name.

My name is Marissa Finn. I live in Minneapolis, Minnesota, with my little peanut dog, Yuri (yes, he has a bow tie AND a Mohawk) and my ridiculously handsome husband, William. You can find us in our tiny house in the city, binge-watching cooking shows, ordering pizza at midnight because we get hungry from watching said cooking shows, and organizing the closets (HA! Kidding. I'm the messiest person ever). All the people we love are a hop, skip, and a jump away from us, and we wouldn't have it any other way. This is the beautiful life that we have fought hard to keep simple—the beautiful life that has been mine for years, but I didn't even realize because I wouldn't let myself stop and enjoy it.

This book is for the beautiful souls who DESERVE the balance of creating their dream life and life itself—the people who feel in their bones that *there has to be more*, and they're willing to do what it takes to get there.

For five years in my twenties, I had enough weekends off work to count on one hand. I was constantly exhausted, burned completely out, and resented every aspect of my life, including myself. Even more crazy is that I was telling everyone (including myself) that I was living my dream life, that I was *thriving*, and that I was happier than ever. In reality, I was depressed, struggling with an eating disorder, losing my relationship, and so anxious I couldn't stand to live in my own skin.

At my tipping point, I had a decision to make: throw in the towel completely or get my shit together and own my damn life.

I chose the second.

So, my question for you: are you ready? Like…really ready? Ready to take the jump into the unknown of your dream life? Ready to make the decision to do something cool with your life? Something meaningful? Something exciting?

Then let's fucking go.

You are meant for more. Straight up. In fact, you're meant to move mountains, win hearts, influence minds, and look damn good doing it. And the awesome thing? All it takes is one shift—one moment when you decide it's finally your turn. Your life. Your dream. It's that simple.

Everything you want can be yours. And trust me, I ALWAYS thought that was straight bullshit when I heard people say it. Anyone who claimed something outrageous like that instantly lost credibility with me, because I always thought there was *no way in hell* achieving a dream was that simple. But it is. If you're willing to fight for it.

I believe my purpose is to tell my story—to share the

unapologetic, socially unacceptable truths about chasing after your dreams and what that truly looks like. For years, I went through hell and back so I could use my experience to empower others by sharing about my massive mistakes that fucked me over.

I started my business at the age of twenty-two. I was a green, inexperienced, naïve twenty-something, all bright-eyed and bushy-tailed, who still slept with a night light, laughed at memes on social media, and spent her free time scouring the Internet for cute fuzzy socks and yummy candles. A twenty-something with a dream. A big dream.

But along the way, shit threw me off course. I made mistakes from which I learned A LOT. I experienced the highest highs and the beyond-lowest lows. I learned what it was like to actually chase a dream with everything inside me. And most of what I learned is the shit that no one talks about out loud—the shit no one tells you about the road to your dream life. The shit that's not socially acceptable to talk about.

As someone who has walked into the dark place, set up camp, survived off rations for three years, and made it out in one piece, I'm pleased to tell you all about how I settled for what I thought others wanted from me, how I held back because I didn't fully believe that I could do it, how I played it safe so I wouldn't have to take the big jump to avoid failure, how I table-flipped my life upside down and managed to land right-side up again.

Here's the deal. WAY too many kick-ass people are settling. They're going through the motions of what they "should" be doing, and what is "smart and reasonable" to do, instead of doing what is RIGHT to do. They're settling for the boss who constantly pisses them off, the job that they don't love, the people they *tolerate* in their life (but secretly want to push over in heels), and the structure of their life that doesn't align with who they are and what they actually want. And by "they," I could very easily mean YOU, sparky. But you wouldn't be here if it wasn't you, now, would you?

So, what I'm about to say might piss you off, but it's time. It's time someone gave it to you straight—no chaser. It's time to take what you deserve, finally. And it's time to start living life on your own terms, all while being PREPARED and READY for what's ahead.

Spoiler alert. This is not a book about all the sunshine and bubbles I experienced on the way to chasing my dream. It's the real, raw, middle-of-the-night stuff. The hard stuff.

This is the book I wish I had read before taking the jump.

Looking back, if someone had told me all the nitty-gritty-shitty stuff, I wouldn't have been unmotivated and scared to go after my dreams. I would have been PREPARED. I would have felt ready to walk through the fire with some-one next to me saying, "Okay, it's going to suck for a little bit, and then a little bit more, and it's going to be hot, and your feet are going to sweat, and you're going to get blis-ters, which then you'll put Band-Aids on, but then those

Band-Aids are going to fall off (and you'll repeat that process several times), and you're going to be scared sometimes, and stressed, and worried, and you will have to keep pushing forward to get through it, but once you do—life gets SO DAMN GOOD!"

It's time to suit up. Because I think being prepared is better than being all filled up with fluff.

Inspiration is fabulous, and I'll give you a solid dose of that throughout these pages, but having REAL and UNDERSTOOD and TRUTHFUL expectations will get you much farther, faster.

This book is meant to share it all: the good, the bad, the dirty, and the ugly. And my hope is that you take these stories and apply them toward your dream life so you can learn from the mistakes that set me back—the mistakes that threw my whole life spinning out of control—and avoid making the same mistakes yourself.

People are going to tell you, "Chase your dreams. It'll be so much fun. You'll be so happy and successful!" But they're leaving out some *very* important pieces of the puzzle that just might be the difference between you throwing in the towel or achieving your wildest dreams.

So, I'm going to tell you all of it. It's going to get ugly. But we're going to get through it together. And by the end, you'll not only be really freaking ready to go after your biggest dreams, but you'll have an insane leverage. You'll know the roadblocks and be equipped to plow right through them. You'll not only make it to that dream life, but it will be so much better than you ever could have imagined.

Let's fucking do it.

CHAPTER 1

Find What Turns You On

Okay, people, this is it. This is where it all began. Let's dive right in, shall we?

I graduated from college with a major (after switching it multiple times because...college) in Communications: Leadership and Advocacy, with a double minor in English and Public Relations, because it sounded really fucking pretty. But in reality, I had no idea what all those majors and minors run together actually meant, or what I could realistically do with them out in the "real world."

I took the classes on my to-do-in-order-to-graduate list, loved most of them, met some really awesome people, and graduated with a shiny bachelor's degree. And yes, I just described my accomplishments in college in one sentence. They don't tell you that eventually it becomes all that work reduced to one single sentence. The most life-changing, seemingly most important years of your life boiled down to a simple summary.

Raise your hand if you, too, went through the struggle of not knowing exactly what you wanted to do at the age of twenty. I'll wait... Raise them higher for the people in the back!

After college, I decided to step into the corporate world, wear heels and power suits, and kick ass up the corporate ladder. With my impressive college education, I could do just about anything. The corporate world seemed like the big stage I needed—and deserved!

Until I got there.

Putting in seventy-hour weeks, I worked my ass off, walking the walk (in my heels, of course) and saying things like "status" and "let's talk offline" and "circle back Monday morning." Repeating this corporate jargon secretly made me want to throw up the salad I would force myself to eat for lunch every day because my daily exercise consisted of walking to the coffee machine and reaching into my drawer to grab my desk snacks.

I felt stuck in a rhythm that I hated. A day-to-day grind that made me unhappy. And I *knew* this wasn't what I truly wanted to do with my life, but I felt I "had to" in order to get a base of experience (you know…to build The Resume). I had *The Feeling*, as too many twenty-somethings do when they first dip their toes into something new, only to figure out that it's not what they thought they wanted all along.

I remember the day I officially decided to quit like it was yesterday. I walked back to the office from lunch, through the gorgeous halls with the high ceilings and linoleum floors, hearing the "click clack" of my heels, overlooking the Minneapolis skyline that I knew I took for granted. This nauseous feeling raged in the pit of my stomach, and I dreaded going back to the office. I felt out of breath, trapped, stuck, agitated, angry, done. I needed to get out that very second.

I loved the office, I loved the people, but I hated the job. I couldn't do it for a second longer.

As soon as I sat back down in my office chair, I started building an exit-plan, how I would quit my job, and what I could do next so that I wouldn't have this feeling again.

I've always been a take action NOW kind of person (as you'll figure out rather quickly in the chapters ahead), and I decided that in order to justify leaving my stable, pretty job, I needed to do something that I loved. And the one thing I loved since the age of three? Dance.

Growing up, I trained in a pre-professional studio: ballet, contemporary, tap, jazz, lyrical, musical theatre—all of it.

Instead of play dates with my friends as a child, I was at the ballet barre. And I wouldn't have had it any other way. Dance was my oxygen. My life.

During the summers for seven years, I worked at a dance company that held workshops all across the country for high school dance teams. Over 1,000 dancers would attend these four-day camps, and I was one of the crazy, high-energy instructors who taught dance all day from 7 a.m. until 10 p.m. I did this job all summer, touring the country, with about two days off every month. And I *loved* it.

But the thing I loved most about it was the choreography, the creating of dances that these dancers would fall in love with and perform for an audience. That was the part that fueled me. That was what I left behind for the corporate world.

So, after a LOT of overthinking, and a good portion of Chinese takeout, I decided to quit my job and start my own choreography company, working IN my passion, while being my own boss, encompassed in an industry I had loved my whole life. I decided to build the exact business that I wanted to work for. I decided to design my life.

I felt a pull that I needed to start this business of my dreams, to just go for it. I wish I could explain that pull better. I wish I could somehow put that feeling into words to show you that there is such a thing as making a huge decision that changes your entire life based on intuition. But I did. And I worked my ass into the very late hours of the night (and usually into the early hours of the morning), on top of my seventy-hour weeks at my corporate job, until I had everything lined up to launch. And that's the real magic of chasing your dreams…doing the not-so-glamorous shit to get there.

But during that time, little by little, things started to look more realistic. I started seeing more aspects of the business that could work, and I was diving into research to figure out the aspects that didn't fully make sense to me. Step by step, day by day, things started to come together in my head—going from a half-baked idea to a fully baked, ready-to-be-served pasta dinner.

Well, one month later, I launched. Yes. You read that correctly. One month. Just like that.

I quit my corporate job and took the jump into the entrepreneurial world.

I spent one month of late nights, early mornings, LOADS of research, planning, editing, designing, and building a potential target client base to start my own choreography company, working with high school and college dance teams. I worked non-stop, living off coffee and Lay's potato chips.

Allow me to explain how the dance team season works before we get any further. High schools and colleges hold tryouts in April, to then work all summer on their routines and training, to compete in the winter at local competitions and nationals until their season ends in February. Peak choreography season is June through September. The four months that would dictate my life for the years ahead.

Here's how I structured my new business. I travel and work with a team for two to three days, teaching them their competition routine for the season. I then leave them to work on that routine for the remainder of the season with their coach, traveling to the next team in a new city, new state—living out of suitcases in hotels, with airports serving as my home office for four months out of the year. I created the best job in the world for myself because I get to work with teams on their most exciting day of the year—the day they learn the routine that sets the tone for their entire season. And as a risk junkie, I enjoy the pressure of having a big part of their season rest on my shoulders by designing and executing an epic routine in a day or two. It gives me a creative high, fulfilling to say the least.

But I wanted my company to be different. I wanted my work to mean something after I left the teams. Choreography and training weren't enough for me. I wanted to empower the industry to start empowering each other. I wanted to turn a highly competitive, cutthroat, toxic world of (mostly) women into a supportive community of badass bosses who *knew* they could do anything.

You see, the dance world is not the real world. At least, I didn't used to see it that way. I saw it as a world filled with coaches who spent their time working on the perception their team was giving off on the outside, investing in the most expensive costumes and warm-ups, training their dancers to walk into competitions with their noses in the air—intimidating their competition in any way possible. Putting on fake smiles while simultaneously giving the side-eye. I saw it as an industry smothered with the notion that, as a coach, as long as you were winning, you could treat your team however you deemed necessary. An industry that was training dancers to focus on the win, focus on the individual award, and not the notions of teamwork, support, and healthy competition. The gossiping was brutal, but what the teams projected to the dance world when they stepped out of practice was even worse. I hated what it had become.

To me, dance was never just a sport. I saw the power, the impact that it had on the humans inside the sport. And I knew I could start a movement to create positive change, to show these dancers and coaches that there was so much more to this sport than the toxic energy that consumed it. Because it is possible to coach a national winning team and never raise your voice. It is possible to teach young humans how to be competitive, while still supporting their rivals. It is possible to change the concept of what it means to be a successful, winning team. And it is possible to intensely train dancers from a voice of motivation instead of fear.

I saw the gap. And it was about damn time someone filled it.

Seeing the desperate need for this in the industry, I knew I had what it took to make it happen, to switch the narrative. The dance world stereotypes are real, and the further you get into the industry, the more you see them come to life full-force. This was my fire, the passion that burned inside me, enough to put my whole heart into a company that would open the conversation, change the narrative, and start a movement.

About two weeks before my launch, I read about an opportunity to attend a dance team conference as a vendor. These conferences pop up every year, usually during the fall season. This conference had over fifty dance teams across the state in attendance. I knew it was my shot, and I knew I had to take it. Everything in me was telling me to go.

So, naturally, without blinking, I skipped my student loan payment that month and put the three hundred dollars toward paying for a booth at that conference. I didn't have money to pay for decorations at the booth, so I bought a cheap black table cloth (which wasn't big enough to fit the whole table), seventy business cards (which came with a typo front and center), and a bunch of sparkly plastic gems to put on the top of the table (because, after all, I was going to a dance team conference. That world does sparkles and they do them BIG). I wanted something that would catch people's eyes as they walked by.

And of course, I brought my mom...for obvious reasons.

I was scared shitless that first day. As the doors opened in the morning, I was so sure that people could smell the fear on me. But I marched on anyway, saying a huge hello to everyone who came even twenty feet from my booth.

I was scrappy. I was resourceful. I inserted myself into every single conversation I could, and I was way over-the-top obnoxious about the promise of my new company. I made it "cool" just by saying that it was cool. I gave something that hadn't even launched yet: ENERGY. And after sixteen hours of that in two days, it worked. Because I did every single second of those sixteen hours with fucking enthusiasm. I approached it with "Well, I don't have a choice. I *have to* book clients." Zero filter. And no, it wasn't cute.

But I truly believed in what I was selling, and I made that quite clear. Crazy loony clear.

I booked seventeen clients at that conference: $50,000 in profit that I would see in the next month. And a month later, I did it again: $100,000 in two months, when two months prior, I couldn't even afford the three-hundred-dollar entry fee into the conference.

I sold the idea of a company that didn't even exist yet, a company that wouldn't launch for two weeks after that conference, off of an electricity that I shared with every single person who crossed paths with me that weekend.

I found it. The thing that turned me on. The thing that I could get fully on board with, flip my whole life for, take the big risks for, go completely broke for. The thing that I wanted to put in the work for. The thing that could keep me up for days on end. The thing that, to me, finally fucking mattered.

IT'S TIME

It's time you stopped waiting for permission and started living a life that makes you really fucking excited to get out of bed in the morning. Don't do what makes you happy in the moment. Do what makes you so pumped that even on your worst mornings, the mornings of stress-induced wine hangovers, rolling out of bed in the same clothes you've worn for three days straight, you are still excited as hell to do what you do (after some coffee, of course). Do something that you can connect to, that you feel a true purpose toward, because that is what will get you through the hard times in building it.

Right now is a pivotal time. People have the freedom to do anything, start anything, just by using the phone at their fingertips. Society has more resources than it ever has, making going after your dreams easier than ever before. You have no excuse. It's time for you to take the damn jump and *just start.*

But here's the thing, taking that jump and being a dreamer—a doer—is scary. There's a lot at stake, most of which is probably already scaring you out of doing it in the first place.

You're always going to have way more reasons (and yes, your teachers, parents, friends, and the thoughts in your own mind are very much some of those) not to go after your dream life than to go after it. But that's why you're here, right? Because you're fucking ready. You've decided.

And now, you want to be prepared.

So, what happened next? Allow me to be blunt.

For two years, I busted my ass. I took the words "grind" and "hustle" to a whole new level. I lost most of my friends, relationships that I truly cared about, missed so many family events I stopped counting, and was constantly traveling across the country. Now, don't get me wrong. In the moment, I was having the time of my life. I loved getting to use the phrase "hustling for my dream." And the messed-up part about it all was that I was obsessed with being busy. I was obsessed with telling people, "I can't. I have a client." My work was fun. Riveting. Addicting. And ultimately, it ruined everything. We'll chat about that later. Can't give away all the goods right away.

Five years later, I decided it was time to share the ugly part of my story, including how, even after the ruinous part, I made it work for me.

This book is not about my business story. It's about my fuck-ups. It's about the uphill, thousand-mile climb with only a bag of nuts and a juice box—and the shit no one told me about truly following my dreams.

Now, you can take my story in one of two ways: She's a whiny diva who doesn't want to work hard in the corporate world and jumped ship the moment she stopped liking it, or she's the woman who had no idea what she wanted to do with her life, so she experimented, tasted everything, took a LOT of wrong turns, made the scary jump, and found something that felt better than she could have imagined—until she learned how to do it right, of course. The woman I am today is here to tell you the truth about going after your dream life—the socially unacceptable things no one else will actually say out loud.

Bottom line: I learned that by doing and trying many things when I first started out, I was able to discover what actually turned me on. I found out what made me get out of bed in the morning and shout to the Universe, "I AM FUCKING HERE!" You will never find what the Universe, God, Mother Nature, Beyoncé is calling you to do unless you test out the waters a little.

Your dream life, your purpose, could be just on the other side of what you think you are meant to do. But it might take hopping a fence and stepping in some dog shit to get there.

Go ahead and call me on this until you figure out it's actually true: You go through all the golden shit for a reason. And that reason is not happening to you; it is happening *for* you (as you'll read in the chapters ahead).

I haven't blocked out the nauseating season when I climbed the mountain. And I'm not above sharing it all, because there are too many people in your boat who need this story—who need the golden nuggets about the golden shit. And the Universe decided it was going to have a little fun with me first and see how much it could screw with me before I got to feel the feeling of freedom and success in my business.

Along the way, I learned that finding my purpose required me to taste all the shit, to try all the things. Once that hit me, I had more clarity than I ever thought possible about my direction. I could breathe again. I felt free, alive, and vibrant. A few years in, I remember looking in the mirror thinking with shock, "Is this really me?" I couldn't BELIEVE IT. I became the woman I was once jealous of, the woman who had control, the woman capable and worthy of anything she set her mind to.

All because I jumped.

Here's the deal: Once you find what you're supposed to do in the world, you feel something click. And no, it's not your neck from sleeping on your friend's futon for weeks because you can't afford rent. And no, it's not your stomach from the bad leftovers you ate because in your drunken stupor you forgot to put it in the fridge when you got home. It's a click of alignment that, all of a sudden, your life makes sense. All of a sudden, you know what you're supposed to do.

You found what turns you on.

Now, don't get it twisted. You are not now magically going to pursue your purpose, and go after your dreams, and life is going to be grand and big and beautiful with champagne toasts, sushi on the beach, and a lavish collection of shoes. The next step you take, the next jump, might just be the stepping-stone to get you to that dream that will give you all the things. This step might not be the thing, but just a little nudge toward the thing, or a pain-in-the-ass lesson you have to learn first. But, if there's anything I learned from jumping and jumping and feeling like a more than half-insane person constantly, it's that the clicks, the feelings of alignment happen for a reason. So, when the click happens, follow it. Seize that dream with everything you have, commit to it, do what you need to do to fully embrace it, and see where it takes you.

Sometimes, it's baby steps. Sometimes, it's getting hit by a two-by-four. And sometimes, it is a seemingly impossible dream that becomes real—a dream that even in your craziest visions for the future, you never thought would come true.

You are made to live your dream life. That is why you're here! And you will never, ever, ever get there if you don't take some risks, make some impulsive decisions, and test out the waters. The beauty of your existence is that even when something isn't your true life's purpose, it is somehow going to connect you to your actual purpose down the line.

Trust that.

DON'T GIVE UP

Here's the issue. Too often, people see the next shiny thing, the next cool job, the next cocktail hour with their girl-friends, hearing about how their lives sound so much better than their own, as a nudge to throw in the towel. When things get hard, instead of pushing through to the other side, they give up and go after the next thing that's not serving them and is just a temporary fix. They start the side hustle, only to abandon it two months later. They launch the blog, only to realize that writing is hard. And they commit to the next "easy way out," because they're easily sold on the notion that success can be quick and painless.

My advice: Know the difference between hard, purposeful work, and work that's not serving you. Period. I've learned there's a difference between having to work hard at something you're aligned to and that you feel is filling your heart—even when things get tough—and quitting or settling because it's not serving who you are. Instead, it's making your life miserable.

What I'm saying is, don't be that person. Don't be the one who quits because it's hard work. You have to be willing to sweat, lose sleep, do the hard shit, and make sacrifices. I'm not saying you have to give away your first child and live on the streets to follow your dream. Be the one who knows the difference. The one who's willing to put in the work without sacrificing your entire life. That's all.

YOU DO YOU. PERIOD.

You get one shot at this life. And the beauty of it is that you get a lot of mini shots within that one shot. Your first decision for a career is not your final decision. You have choices. And you owe it to yourself to make the hard ones.

College does not dictate your life. It is a choice in which you have many options. It is not some magic gateway into the dream life like all the pretty pamphlets say. You create your own dream life. Whatever you want it to be. We need to stop putting so much weight into something that is an *elective* decision. Because more and more, people are starting to pursue careers without a college degree, and that makes sense for them.

Your job isn't to go to college because you feel obligated by society. Your job is to find your purpose, to try everything until you find what you can get excited about. For a lot of people, that purpose stems from college. But if college is not calling you, DON'T GO.

My major in college felt like I was put in a bucket, like I was a communications major and I needed to do something "impressive" *in that field* because I invested so much money toward my degree. I felt like there was this "Grand Plan" created for my life by everyone around me. Professors and advisors and counselors and family members talk about the options in that field, but NO ONE is talking about what happens if you graduate, find a job in your designated field, and then decide you don't like that field in which you just invested $100,000…

And I get it. It's the job of the people around you in college to support you in the major that you are working so hard toward, but we need to start bringing to surface the aftermath of choosing a career outside of that major.

Guess what, people? You change A LOT from the age of eighteen to twenty-two. A lot. And I'm here to spit the truth. It's completely normal to not settle for a job within the realm of your degree that you actually hate but feel obligated to. You are meant to thrive in a career that makes you feel joy and happiness and excitement, not a career that you feel tied to because of a very expensive piece of paper.

There is absolutely nothing wrong with experimenting with things in your life. By all means, date ALL the types, try ALL the face creams, and do things that actually interest you. You can either have a sexy, spicy life, or you can live in the hole you've dug yourself because, for one reason or another, you refuse to go after the thing that excites you the most. This is your time. Your life. Your joy. Do NOT give it away to the thing for which society is telling you to settle.

The danger lies in staying in something you hate for WAY too long, only to waste years of your life, finding out later that it's causing you anxiety, a bad sex life, and overall, a rager of a pity party. There's a difference between putting in the work that sucks, but is necessary, and trudging along for years in something you hate, mistaking it for "hard work and dedication."

You do you, boss.

GO FOR IT.

The mindset that allowed me to take jumps in my career and my life was this: Due to the college payment system,

I will be in mind-numbing debt for the next fifteen years anyway, so why the hell not?

When I first started my business, I was in the hole $50,000. Yes, you read that number right. And the money in my bank account to live and survive in my day-to-day? Less than two hundred dollars. When I say I was broke, I truly mean broke. I was post-college, pre-figured-out-my-life broke. And yes, this was with a full-time corporate job…

I looked into starting my business by doing what all good souls do when they don't know something. I took to Google.

On a rainy spring day in the middle of April, I typed "how to start a business in the state of Minnesota" into my search bar. After sifting through what felt like an obscene amount of unnecessary paperwork, I found the price: $135 to file with the Secretary of State.

That price stopped me dead in my tracks, because I knew I couldn't make rent that month if I decided to start my business. So, as I climbed into my bed to sulk and feel sorry for myself, I saw a piece of mail lying on the end table that I hadn't yet opened. It was an ad for an American Express credit card.

In that moment, I knew I had a choice. Either wait to start my business until I had the money in cash, or follow the itching, explosive feeling that was telling me to activate that credit card and start the business NOW.

So, naturally, I activated the card. And I leveraged the hell out of it to survive. Groceries, rent, gas, shampoo…everything. I did this until my first invoice went through, which paid off the entire card and then some.

Figure out a way to make your dream work for you. Just figure it out. Period. "But I have this and this and this…" Nope. Figure it out. It is absolutely possible.

Working ninety-hour weeks for a month and leveraging a credit card to start my business was how I did it. And looking back, it did the trick. But you have to do what is right for you and what will drive you forward. If all of your insides are telling you to take action NOW and you have The Feeling, then make it work somehow. Because there is always, always, always a way. Sometimes, you just have to get creative to find it.

If you don't go for it now, if you don't relentlessly look for the things that excite you and turn you on, then when? The crushing reality is that too many people never do. And if nothing else has registered with you so far, I am going to go here and then we're going to breeze right past it: Do you want to be old and look back on your life with regret about all the things you didn't do? Or, will you look back at all the things you did, then utterly failed at, but then learned from—all bringing you closer to the things that allowed you to *live*?

I choose the second option.

The story of my many attempts to find what I really love to do isn't widely considered a positive thing, but I'm sharing it because if you're reading this book, you're likely at a vital, pivotal point in your life (because aren't we all, always?). Too many people think they're backed into a corner in their careers, whether that's how they perceive themselves, or how they perceive other people perceive them. The stories you've told yourself about why you don't deserve your dream life, or why you think you need to settle and not try out plenty of options aren't true.

Read that last sentence again.

Experimenting with your career is not just important; it's necessary. Trying and failing and trying again (multiple times) is the single thing that separates those who live a vibrant life that they've created for themselves, and those who live their life as "good enough," never even realizing the other side of the reality they've settled for.

There are a million jobs in the world. And the best part: If you browse through the catalogue and don't see what you're looking for, you can *create your own*. That's what I did, and I'm here to tell you it is absolutely, 100 percent possible. Ask yourself honestly, "If I could do absolutely anything with my life, and learn everything along the way, what would I do?" No buffer, no filter, just answer.

Your "thing" might not be the thing you are good at. You need to stop looking there. If you could sit down with a guru in the field that turns you on, and they could teach you everything there is to know about getting there, what would that one thing be?

And my guru? Google.

I chose to launch a choreography and consulting company because I was good at it and I loved the work. It came super easy to me, and many people admired my work, which made me excited. The more I thought about it, the more excited I became, because I thought that I had finally found my path. I had to do it because I would have regretted it if I didn't. I took my shot. And being the stubborn pain-in-the-ass that I am, I am thankful that I stuck it out.

I proved to myself that I can do hard things. I can build a six-figure business in two months, one client at a time. I can go an entire week on ten hours of sleep. And I can do just about anything in the world if I am overly caffeinated.

Throughout the first year, I had a crazy spark. I was freaking pumped all the time. That year was constantly exciting, and my business was constantly changing and evolving into something better. It was the momentum I needed to start it all.

I felt alive. I felt free. I felt connected.

Follow the ideas that keep you up at night. The ideas in your head are there for a reason. You can very easily get away with the impulse decisions that end up being epic failures, because it was all in pursuit of your dreams. I'm not saying go crazy. You still have a brain, and I think it's wise for the sake of the rest of the world that you use it. But if you are choosing to use that brain to overthink everything and never truly go for it, then you are wasting your beautiful life.

You deserve to constantly be in pursuit of your spark, your passion, what lights you up inside. And your future deserves you doing whatever it takes to get there.

Take some time to figure out what is calling to you—what turns you on. Then go after it.

Oh, but Marissa, it can't be that simple.

Oh, but it is.

Taste all the shit. Dive in head first. Take to Google.

Keep reading.

CHAPTER 2

Do the Work

When I first launched my choreography company, I kept thinking that the hardest part was over. I kept thinking that taking the initial jump was going to be the kicker. That everything that came after would be way easier. Now, here comes the shit no one tells you about chasing after your dreams. The hardest part is NOT in taking the initial jump. The hardest part is the work that comes after. The middle part between the jump and the top of the mountain.

Here is where it gets interesting.

Picture this: I'm sitting outside a coffee shop at one of those cute tables with the umbrellas, my best friend Tia by my side (because she's my ride-or-die, badass boss business babe). We're having our fancy lattes and enjoying the sunshine. It's the season in Minnesota where everyone goes outside and practically lives there because we only get a couple of months of it. I have my computer open, ready to hit launch on my website and announce my new business on social media, with the sun shining brightly in my face. I'm sweating, shaking with nerves, and chugging espresso.

I take a deep breath, close my eyes, and hit launch. Just like that.

As the texts, calls, and messages of support came flooding in, I remember thinking, "This is so exciting! I'm a business owner now. I can do anything!" My chest puffed up, my head held high, and my diva pants on.

That night, I popped champagne in my sweatpants with my boyfriend (now husband, Will) in our little backyard, and we celebrated the start of it all.

I woke up the next day, coming down from my high. And suddenly, it dawned on me as I opened up my computer to get to work that even though I invested so much time and energy planning for this launch, and in my head had everything prepared, I had no idea what the fuck I was doing.

I have been a book-a-week reader since college. Before my launch, my topics of choice for six months were business, marketing, online presence, finances, and anything that had to do with starting a business. That stuff interested me even before I made the decision to start my business, and I always wanted to learn about how businesses come together. I read about systems and saving and social media funnels and customer service and a million other topics. I felt so prepared going into that launch, yet when it happened, I was a lost puppy the second I got to work.

Now, don't go thinking that I had nothing set in place. I give myself a tiny bit more credit than that. I had what the pretend experts call a semi-system (meaning, a half-assed system that, in theory, could potentially work—but there was no proven method, so, therefore, it was a crooked shot in the dark). I was so disorganized, it was scary. But I did have one thing…an entire database of over eight hundred potential clients that I had collected before the launch. My plan was to email/message/call/pigeon carrier every single one of those clients and sell my services to them.

And so, for the next two weeks, that is all I did. Fifty clients a day, each one a personalized message directed specifically toward them explaining how my company was different and how I could serve them. I went at this with more energy and enthusiasm than I have gone after anything in my life. I was a machine. A fearless, cold-calling maniac. And you know what?

It worked.

If anyone tries to tell you that there's such a thing as being prepared before you launch a business and jump full-force into your dream, they are bold-faced lying to you. Even if you think you're prepared, I hate to break it to you, but there are things that fall through the cracks. Always. When I first started out, no one told me there's a distinct difference between feeling prepared and actually being prepared. The minute I pressed GO, I felt prepared. But the day after I launched, curve balls came flying right at me for the next three years, most of them knocking me in the face. If I had known that was going to happen, I would have been better prepared for the flying balls. In fact, I would have had a big butterfly net ready to catch them all.

So, my dear friends, know that there will be flying balls. Know that doing the work to feel prepared is important. And trust that you will need to walk directly into the shit storm of a launch while also dodging flying balls to get through to the other side. You will not be prepared enough for what the universe has planned. And that's normal.

I recommend a butterfly net.

One single thing saved me and gave me crazy momentum on post-launch day when I felt like a total failure and a lost puppy disaster. This one action picked me up just before I lost my mind, switching back and forth from thinking, "Jesus, take the wheel! What the hell am I doing? I have no business starting a company! I am such a fraud. How do I get my old job back?" to "Well, shit. I better figure this out." I did what every beautiful soul starting a business and having no idea what they are doing does. I went on Google and typed, "How to effectively cold call and retain new clients." And from there, my journey to success began.

If you're wondering if I'm a manic, crazy psycho who can't get her emotions in check, I am not. Mostly. Because jumping into something huge requires you to go from feeling like you can take on the world with nothing but a good eyelash day, to feeling like the entire Universe is falling apart, all within a couple of seconds.

Seconds.

Throughout the first two months of starting, I literally thought I could do anything. I wasn't even hitting that level of success in a business that was widely known and could attract diverse clients from all over the world. I was targeting one of the most niche audiences out there—high school and college dance team coaches in the United States with school budgets that could afford, allow, and wanted outside choreographers to come in. That meant only about twenty people in each state, if that. Making that amount of money and having that much success in my first two months with zero network of potential clients and reach was miraculous. I actually, to this day, am shocked that it happened.

But after those first few months of crazy, when the dust settled and I could take a breath, I started putting together the details as to how my business would actually run. I started piecing together the things that I knew nothing about when starting a business. The branding. The messaging. The front that my clients would see.

Side note, and this is important: It is possible to start a business with all of the details still floating around. All you need is good customer service and a client base. I've learned that the rest, no matter how important it might seem, is trivial at the start. And that, I firmly believe. I lived it.

Furthermore, I understood the concept of setting myself apart to grow a niche business, and I took that and ran with it. I started scaling drastically when I took the risk and did something no other choreography company was doing. I presented myself as their assistant coach for the season. Meaning, I created a full experience, and I signed on for the season, making myself available to their every need.

My messaging: *I'm here for tiny tweaks in choreo* (an industry abbreviation for choreography…just in case)*, late night phone calls, and pump-up video sessions during practice.*

I made them feel like I was sitting down having a latte with them, instead of talking cost. I made it about girl talk, and we chatted about THEIR lives, not their team. I asked questions, and instead of talking about my services, we talked about their kids and their love lives and their new living room decor and how they like their coffee.

And by approaching my business like I was approaching a girls' getaway weekend, I learned that everyone just wants to be heard, to be understood, to feel human connection. They don't want to be sold to; they want to be related to. They want to feel like you're on their team. They want to know that you're a friend they can trust with their prized possession, and in my clients' case, the team that they put countless hours into every day after their full-time jobs, the team they've built over years of hard work and late nights of wine and headaches. Their team whom they love.

I made myself available for texting, emailing, video chatting, and calling every single second of the day and night. Their problems were my problems. Their team was now my team, who I cared for just as much as they did. I held on so tight to my clients who didn't need/expect me to. I took them by surprise in an industry where this type of connection with a consultant doesn't exist. I set myself apart.

And by doing that, I scaled.

WHAT NOT TO DO

The level to which I built my business was created out of hard fucking work. And by work, I mean the kind where your business becomes your ENTIRE life—you lose friends, get completely burned out, become a gigantic stress ball, and can't get turned on sexually because you never stop thinking about work. In fact, the person inside you dies. You turned her into a machine.

Fast-forward to the end of year two. I managed to double my income by working eighty-hour weeks, not having a single weekend off in two years, all while completely tanking my relationships with my friends, my boyfriend (now husband, who stuck with me through the mess and is the real fucking rock star here), and my own mind.

Meet The Dark Place.

I went through a period during year two when I didn't sleep for two months. I couldn't shut my brain off. I would lie in bed and replay songs over and over in my head, or I'd fixate on conversations that happened throughout the day. I couldn't fall asleep. I assumed that I had some kind of sleeping disorder, as anyone does when she can't sleep and refuses to take responsibility.

It got so bad that one night, I woke up to my chest hurting, my hands numb, and my breath short—so short that I actually couldn't breathe.

I was having a panic attack.

I'll spare you the details of how Will and I sat on our bathroom floor crying from fear. How the only thing we thought to do was breathe into a paper bag (saw it in a movie once). How I actually thought I was dying. And how, at the time, a part of me would have been at peace with that.

I truly hit what I thought was the bottom. Oh, how I was underestimating the depth of the bottom…

I went to the doctor, hoping that he would tell me something magical that would make it all go away so I could sleep again. Instead, he gave me sleeping pills and told me to lower my stress level.

That was the first time I actually scratched the surface in realizing just how deep in the water I had sunk. I left the doctor appalled that he told me to lower my stress level. *Didn't he know I was running a business?!*

For all of you business owners who have thought the same thing, I empathize. I get it. Because it does feel like you have the most important job in the entire world and no one could possibly understand because you are the one constantly treading the water and fighting the fight. There's nothing that could possibly make it easier or lower your stress level because you have made it past the point of no return. I became the psychopathic, maniac boss-lady running the streets. I needed a glass of wine and a sleeping pill to calm my shit so I could sleep for five hours a night. I was so stressed I was scaring the dog. And that is NEVER an acceptable level of stress (a moment of regret for my little monster).

My advice looking back? Fucking breathe. And do NOT do what I did.

MAKE A CONSCIOUS DECISION

My mistake was taking my business to the point of no return. I table-flipped my life into a spiraling disaster just to grow my business. Boundaries? Nonexistent. Self-care? That's cute.

And I'm here to tell you there's another way.

You will notice, the more PRODUCTIVE work you put in, the more the stress goes away. What I've found is that most of my stress is a result of teetering the line between knowing what I have to do and actually doing it. Throwing myself into the bullshit of busywork and actually doing the RIGHT work.

Often people know exactly what they need to do; they just don't do it for one reason or another. Your job is to figure out what your reason is for not wanting to put in the work when you get stressed, and then fix it. Triggers, people. Take them to lunch and air it all out.

Feeling overwhelmed? Get laser-focused on one single task. And then, once that's finished, another one. Do this until you reach the moon. Because you will.

The more productive the work, the less volume of work. I live by that.

You are the only thing standing in the way of you and your dream life.

Yes, you.

Make the choice to put in the *actual* work, and watch the stress slowly dissipate.

You need to put in a different kind of work if you truly want your dream life. Simple as that. Your dream life will not happen by simply announcing it to the world. You have to take the necessary steps and put in the time and energy to make it happen. Because when you can show up CONSISTENTLY and put in the right kind of work, the Universe will reward you. If you aren't a Universe, God, Buddha, All-Encompassing Power believer, allow me to rephrase: Doing the right kind of work equates to achieving success.

And there is such a thing as putting in the right kind of work and having a healthy work-life balance.

We'll get to that.

Yes, there will be a trial-and-error period where you make some massive mistakes. But it is possible to scale a company and still take your dog for a walk with your hubby on Saturday morning. Take it from the person who completely lost her life and then regained it. It IS possible to recover from massive mistakes.

You just have to embrace the adjustment period.

The time that comes after you make the decision to put in the work is what will force real momentum into your life. The work is a DECISION that only YOU can make. Your entire life is based on your ability (or inability) to take action toward your dreams. Anyone can jump into starting the journey to their dream life. But not everyone is willing to do what comes after, what bridges the gap between the initial jump and the success.

The work.

THE SECRET WEAPON

Allow me to, once again—because I cannot emphasize this enough—give away the secret to scaling a business with zero knowledge on the subject: Google.

Building and scaling your dream life is a learned art. I tripled my business by typing all of my questions into Google and learning everything I could on the subject. I don't have a business degree. I have a computer with Internet. I promise you will look back and realize that you did not know one single thing about growing a business when you first started. You LEARN it as you go. There is no secret weapon, sauce, or club. And almost every single person who's grown a business will tell you that very same thing.

I read a book a week for months on every single topic of business. I spent weeks developing a sound game plan. I did it all. But once I started, none of that mattered because what I was learning from taking action was so much more valuable than the prep work.

The truth is, you have no idea what you don't know until you dive in. There is no way to prepare. And the secret plan of action that will get you to your dreams faster than anything else?

Work.

THE TYPE OF WORK MATTERS

Let's take a second and talk about the type of work that will actually move the needle forward, the purposeful work.

I break my work into three categories: marketing, communications, and innovation. Marketing refers to anything that attracts potential clients and moves the brand forward. Communications means anything that is client-facing: emails, calls, in-person work. And innovation refers to anything that I do creatively to constantly improve the business.

Notice I did not put a category in there for the silly busy-work, tasks that look pretty but are not actually moving your business forward. I see those as tasks to do off the clock, things that you could realistically hire out for and don't have to touch (but you will in the beginning). When you're in the thick of it, when you're first building, these things aren't your main focus. Yes, there is a time and a place, but in order to move the needle forward, you need to focus on the main three categories.

Now, here is what I do in each of these categories to scale.

Marketing: Creating and pushing out constant content. That's it. I scaled my business solely by creating valuable content from which I knew my clients would benefit. Some was motivational, some were tangible concepts to apply to their work, some were videos of my thoughts after working with clients, some were drills that they could do in practice, and the list goes on. I created the content that I knew my clients would be able to learn from, and I ran with it. I pushed this content out to my email list, social media posts, digital ads, everything. And every once in a while...I sold to them. And by every once in a while, I mean literally never.

I grew my client base one follower, one email subscriber at a time. And those first two months, those first six figures? I had less than two hundred followers and twenty-four email subscribers.

If you're doubting your reach, read that again. One more time. And again, just to be sure that sinks in.

My main goal for marketing was to provide mega value to my potential clients. And the more value I provided, the more clients would sign on because they trusted what I was putting out there. They saw firsthand what I could bring to the table if they hired me. No one had to take a shot in the dark. They knew exactly what they were getting. I treated my new email subscribers/followers the same as potential clients and the same as my highest paying clients. They were all the same to me.

I cared that I wasn't feeding them fluff. Because I was sick of seeing the fluff, and I knew the industry was craving more. These clients wanted resources, new things to try with their teams, and motivation for their dancers that would sink in differently. So, that is what I gave them.

Fuck what everyone is saying about what you should be doing to market your business forward, and just trust your gut. I didn't pay for a single online ad that first year. Every single one of my clients was either from my social media, my email list, or word-of-mouth. And I am damn proud of that.

Provide value and push out content like crazy. That's it.

Serve, serve, serve. And every once in a while, remind them what you are selling.

Communications: I turned the word "client" into "friend." And it changed everything. I treated clients like they were my best friends. I knew what was going on in their lives, and I talked to them like we were friends catching up over a couple of lattes on a Saturday morning. I chose to position myself differently, to immerse myself into everything surrounding them. I knew how many kids each client had, the big things happening in their lives, like buying a house or switching day jobs, and what their purpose was behind coaching—what they loved about it and what their pain points were.

Communication, to me, was easy because I cut down the barrier between the client and the consultant. Instead, it was two friends, chatting about their new winter mittens and their favorite workouts. Will this work in every single industry? No. But most (like almost every single one)? Absolutely.

Clients are people. And they should be treated as such.

Another thing that I did in the communications realm to really push my business forward was to be on top of my messages, always. Unless my away message was on, I responded to every single new inquiry within an hour, and every single email that same day. Because people go in a different direction when they have to wait, and that's just how it is. I didn't give them the time to wait. I made them see that I would be diligent in everything, from the start of our time working together, all the way to the end. The timeliness of my emails was my first impression to them. It is the ONLY thing you can control at the beginning, aside from the messaging… So, I made it count. Do you need to respond to everything right away? No. But does it help in our "instant gratification" society? Abso-freaking-lutely.

Break down the barrier and read what your clients are truly craving. Control what you can with the utmost attentiveness. And yes, that's it.

Innovation: I constantly looked for ways to improve my brand, and once I did, I took action immediately. But I didn't look within the dance world; I looked at every other industry to see how they were being creative. I studied photographers, graphic designers, boutique stores, coffee brands, and I found inspiration by how they branded and set themselves apart. And then I made it my own in the dance industry. I applied that inspiration to my events, my emails, my content, and the way I approached my business as a whole. I took what I liked across so many different industries, flipped it to how I wanted it, and threw the rest out.

You can choose to do this all day long, but if you don't actually implement it into your business, it is a big fat waste of time. I was nervous at first to put out the content I created because it was different than anything I had ever seen in the dance world. But eventually, it set my company apart completely. Clients gravitated to it BECAUSE it was different. I took a risk with a lot of the content I was putting out there, but that's what made it stick. That's how I scaled.

In the innovation world, you HAVE to be different, because now, everyone is putting out the same thing. You have to stand out. And you have to take action. I promise, it's worth it. Think differently, and even after you think it's different, push it twelve steps further.

Now your job is to create a rhythm for all of the categories. Decide how you want to assign your time, and Put. In. The. Work. I created a rhythm that made sense for me week by week. With all of my traveling, I would choose one of my days off to batch work my content for the month, meaning I would be a content-making MACHINE for a full day, and then I would sprinkle in and repurpose that content throughout my different channels where it was needed all month long so I would have time for the other categories in the evening, after my clients, in my hotel room, with my plate of French fries from room service.

Take this and apply it somehow to YOUR dream.

Like, today.

"But, Marissa, my industry is so different. This won't work for me…"

Cute story.

Today.

THE DIRTY WORD

Here, we will talk about the dirty word that ruins the lives of all dreamers who throw themselves into the ring of fire.

BUSY.

There's a BIG difference between doing the work that's going to propel you forward into the life of your dreams and just doing work. You can pluck away at your computer all day, look back over emails you've opened already, organize your inbox, watch inspirational videos, make to-do lists, clean your office, order cool pens, and scroll social media, going all day without actually accomplishing ANYTHING.

If you want to make real shit happen, you have to do real shit. You have to take a hard look at the reality that is your productivity and work structure. It needs to be mandatory to have things on your daily list that move the needle forward. And the beauty of just starting out is that you might not know what those things are just yet. So, take time to learn the things that are going to make your dream life happen, and then actually go and do them.

However, the fatal flaw lies in knowing what those things are, knowing how important they are to do, having every intention to do them, believing with every ounce of yourself that they are going to bring you closer to your dreams, and then *not* doing them, consuming yourself with random other things instead, convincing yourself that the "busy" you are experiencing is driving you toward your dreams.

I once went a whole month without doing any relevant work. I was stuck. I got out of bed every morning and had a whole morning routine. I went to yoga, made myself lunch, reorganized the office, sat in my inbox, maybe posted on social media, and that was it. FOR A MONTH. I was in a tough spot in the year where I knew what I had to be doing, but it seemed at the time that running a marathon would have been easier—and I *hate* running.

I made myself out to be super busy by filling my schedule with meaningless crap that didn't matter. I could have been enjoying a slower season and plucking away at my to-do list, but instead I was spending that time convincing myself I was busy, wasting my energy. And the worst part? I was also convincing everyone else, without even realizing it.

Pay attention to what is making you busy. And figure out if it is worth selling your soul, or if you are glorifying the concept without an actual outcome.

There will be SO many days when you won't want to put in the work. The work is hard. And that's the shit no one tells you when you're starting out. Many people will tell you that if you pursue your passion, everything will fall into place. That you will LOVE going to work every day—easy and breezy—and you'll be so happy because you get to do what you enjoy every day.

Well, I wouldn't be on brand if I wasn't bursting your bubble about this belief. The journey to your dream life doesn't happen like that. Even if you are pursuing your passion, many days you'll wake up dreading the work because you see the mountain. It's high and it's steep and to get up there, you have to get sweaty and messy and dirty and scrappy—that's hard. Some days it's impossible to see the "why" that you started with in the first place. And that feeling is *normal*. Losing sight of your "why" does not mean it's time to quit—that you've lost your passion and you should find something else to do. It just means that you are approaching the next level, the next beast.

What do you do when you approach the beast? Maybe you take a couple of days off. Maybe you put your laptop in the dryer. (Yes, I do this. It helps, but do NOT turn the dryer on. No matter how badly you want to.) And maybe you just need a nice solid kick in the rear to get you up and moving again, because you ARE capable. You just forgot for a hot second.

It's normal to get burned out. It's normal to want to put things off. It's normal to not want to put in the work. It is normal. And we'll get to this hot topic in a couple of chapters, so stick with me.

The problem is that our society has glorified "work" and "being busy" and "stress" so much that we have made joy and happiness the end goal. So, let's not make those experiences the end goal. Let's just put them in the routine. Instead of chasing the carrot of happiness with "busy," imagine you already have the carrot and you're snacking on it as you work your ass off, at a reasonable pace, to get to the next level, whether that's to buy the new house, to travel around Europe, to have a baby, to drink the lattes…

You *can* have it all. But glorifying "busy" instead of doing the real work won't get you there. Pretending you're planning, not procrastinating, won't get you there either. Let's flip the script. Let's get the shit done. Every last bit of it.

THE REALITY OF SUCCESS

You will reach your level of success because you have put in the time and effort. Energy equals outcome. It is an unequal exchange at first, as you will put in so much more energy than what you are getting in return. And you will learn after a while that all of that was necessary. The late nights, early mornings, drowning yourself in coffee, and feeling the roller coaster of emotions nineteen million times a day are all part of the beauty.

I didn't do any fancy stuff. I didn't buy the programs or invest in the courses or sign on for an office or pay for a fancy email list subscription. I did the bare minimum of spending on the things that all the business experts said I "needed" so I could invest in what truly mattered: scaling. I was cheap. And that MATTERED. That made a difference. Simple keeps you focused.

That first year, I hit a level of success I never imagined in my wildest dreams, only because my level of work exceeded what I thought I needed to do to actually hit my goals. I didn't waste time with anything the consumer world of all the business experts was telling me to do/buy. I simply took my level of work past what I thought I needed, and that's when I saw the most success.

And the big secret? I didn't take my foot off the gas when I saw that initial success. I pressed harder on the pedal.

That's how you build a business.

But eventually (sigh of relief), there is a shift. And it becomes equal. You start to see the outcome just as much as the energy you are putting in, and then you see the outcome even MORE than the energy you are putting in. That is when it gets fun. I saw that shift in my third year of business. And no, it shouldn't take that long. Keep reading, friends. The golden shit continues in the chapters ahead.

DON'T FALL INTO THE TRAP.

Every day, you have to remind yourself of what you're after. Because it is SO easy to get distracted. Life happens, you get exhausted, you see shiny things and "quick fixes," and you assure yourself that you can take the easy way out, convincing yourself that you don't need that dream life.

But, my friend, the Universe does a phenomenal job at playing these sick jokes with your brain, testing you to see just how badly you want what you said you did. Do NOT confuse difficult work with *not meant to be,* which is just a fancy way of saying that you gave up on your dreams and settled for a life you didn't want but could tolerate nonetheless.

My best, most successful moments have come from the depths of weeks with minimal showering, constant bed hair, wearing the same sweatpants for a number of days in a row that I am not willing to share, mountains of coffee mugs and packages of sour gummy worms strewn about. Weeks when I didn't care about ANYTHING except putting in the work. Magic is created in the messy times.

Embrace the hot mess and keep pushing forward, because once you come out of those depths, it is going to be really freaking amazing. I created the marketing structure that got me to multiple six figures after a week of peanut butter and jelly sandwiches eaten at my desk and an overflowing garbage can of Diet Coke cans and coffee pods.

Hang tight, team. It's all worth it.

The world is waiting for you. Your stage is set, the crowd is taking their seats, and the lights are dimming. That stage is all yours, as soon as you put in the work.

CHAPTER 3

It's Okay to Force Shit

My mother is the most beautiful woman in the world, radiating both on the outside and the inside. She wears glasses, but you don't even notice them because you never make it past her kind eyes. She is gentle, but fierce. Warm. Brilliant. Encompassing love. She is the kind of person who would go so far out of her way to make sure you are having a good day. The kind of person who gives hugs to strangers, makes sure everyone else is fed before she sits down to eat, will talk to someone she just met for hours and chat through their life problems—fixing every single one, and has a contagious love for life and everything around her. Her hugs feel like home, and her words make you feel welcome, safe, loved, and affirmed. You'll never forget her energy after meeting her. She is kind and luminous and giving of everything she has to the rest of the world. She is an angel in human form. My best friend.

That's why, when she was diagnosed with stage four breast cancer at the age of fifty-five, my world shook. My life stopped. Every single ounce of joy I had in me was sucked out.

Because after she fought like hell for two years with stage three breast cancer, going through innumerable rounds of chemo and radiation and putting her body through the fucking ringer, she was only clear for a year.

And then it came back.

The first time I found out about her cancer, I was away at college. It was the day after my finals. Three finals in one day. Exhausting. Now, if I wasn't a young, naïve, stubborn college student at the time, I would have switched one of my finals to a different day so I didn't have to take them all in one day. Just like my mother told me to do.

I was at the laundromat just down the street (everything was just down the street in that tiny college town, you could walk from one end to the other in an hour or so). I was getting ready to pack up to go home for the summer, transferring my warm clothes from the dryer into my laundry basket, when I got a call from my mom.

All throughout college, we usually talked on the phone

about three to four times a day, as many homesick college students do. I told her everything, so this call was not unexpected or out of the blue. But immediately, I could tell something was off.

I don't remember most of that phone call, but I do remember the, "They found a lump," sentence and the, "I start chemo and radiation soon," sentence. I don't remember how long I stayed silent on the other end, but I do remember sitting on the floor next to the dryer, my clothes half hanging over the side, not being able to breathe.

I can't tell you how I finished packing up, or even how I made it home, because I honestly don't know. I think they call that the Grace of God, or something like that.

I blocked out most of the two years after that call during the most intense part of her treatment. It's funny how our brains can do that; block out the hard stuff so we don't have to revisit it, feel it, pretend it never happened. Denial is easier than pain.

However, one memory stuck, reminding me of how hard she fought constantly.

I was in my corporate internship at the time, living at home and driving the hour to and from work in Minneapolis every day. Most days, I lived in a world where my mom didn't have cancer, as that was easier than accepting reality. I didn't know how to endure the pain of my best friend being in so much pain. So, neglecting that it was real life seemed easier.

But some days, it hit. And when it hit, it hit hard.

It was a long day at the office, and I was lying in bed, still in my power suit, exhausted as hell. My mom knocked softly on the door, as she always did before entering, and came in to ask me about my day.

Tears immediately welled up in my eyes, and I had a painful lump in my throat, trying not to cry in front of her (I always tried at this, but rarely succeeded. Now, I'm a pro.). Her face was so swollen from the chemo that I could barely recognize her, and her burn from the radiation showed just enough over the neckline of her shirt that I could feel it on my own skin.

She tried at small talk until she saw the tears in my eyes. Immediately, she crawled into bed with me and tickled my back, as she always did when I was in pain. But what made my heart break even more was the reality that even through her pain and suffering, she still had it in her to be strong for others—a trait I strive for every single day.

When my mom left the room a half-hour later, it was time to cry. I allowed myself these cry sessions every once in a while, and for the rest of that evening, I buried myself under the blanket in bed and silently cried myself to sleep, just hoping it would end. Praying to anything that would listen. I woke up in my work clothes the next morning and caked on eye makeup so no one at my internship could see my puffy eyes.

That was the morning I decided I would choose resilience over suffering. But through that process, I learned that they were often one and the same.

When she told the family that the cancer came back at stage four, after a year of cancer free, after a year of holding our breaths, I was sitting at the kitchen table with my hands on my legs, just shaking. I was beyond angry. I was the kind of pissed where you just want to throw a chair across the room and scream. I hated the world. I hated the Universe. And all I wanted to do was blame something, anything, for bringing this disease into my sweet mother's life. I wish I used to be the kind of person who didn't wish bad things on the doctors who didn't catch it sooner, but I wasn't. I didn't understand it, and I couldn't possibly get out of my own world enough to see that people make mistakes, even the doctors. But somehow, she could look past it. Because she always, always sees the good in others.

My mother, of all people, the saint that she is, did not deserve this. It made me sick. And all I could fixate on were all the terrible people in the world who never get cancer. The killers and terrorists and rapists who will never experience the pain my mother not only survived, but would have to go through again—this time, a million times worse, if that was even possible for a human to endure.

That was, before I learned how to see the good in people, too.

She sat us all down, the whole fam bam, and told us three

days before my first busy season of traveling, after working my ass off for months to book back to back clients for four months straight. This would be not only my first busy season, but the first time I would travel the country by myself for four months straight. And my mom had fucking terminal cancer.

The truth is, I didn't care at all about my clients after I heard the news. I was ready to call them all and say that I couldn't come, and send them recommendations for another company to use. My company wasn't just something I threw to the wayside. In my mind, it was disposable, because I couldn't function. And in the time that I needed my mom the most, she needed me more to stay strong.

As if I knew how.

I took a day to think about it. I ran through every possible scenario in my head. And I eventually came to the conclusion that I would cancel my clients. I began making a list of people I had to call, and hotels and flights I had to try to cancel and get refunded. And the morning before I was going to call them all, I went over to my parent's house to tell them I was going to be around for the next four months for whatever they needed me for, so my dad could continue working and they wouldn't have to worry about care while she was going through her harsh treatment.

My mom said, "No." That simple. She wouldn't let me do it. And for reasons I still can't wrap my head around, she told me that I wasn't allowed to call off my clients.

My only hope in life is that someday I will be a big enough person to understand how she did what she did. That someday I will share her impossible courage and love so fiercely that other people cannot even comprehend how. My only hope is that someday, I will be half the woman that she is.

Now you must also know that she is just as much of a stubborn asshole as I am. And I knew that if she told me no, that was a life or death answer with a period at the end (she used to work at a law firm. Her no's were solid). I knew I had to do my busy season, despite every single ounce of everything in me totally rejecting it, because she was proud of me. She supported me. Hard.

So, off I went. I traveled to twelve states in four months, and worked with thirty-two brand new clients. I lived out of hotels and airports, and found a way to survive on coffee, day-old mascara, and, once again, the Grace of God. I spent my days blocking it out and kicking ass, and my nights crying in my hotel room. I spent eight to nine hours a day totally in denial of the life that was happening outside of my job, and once that key slid through the lock on the hotel door, I spent the next few hours, before crying myself to sleep, completely consumed with the life that I could not control, and could not believe was happening.

I managed to sustain this for four months. To this day, I have no idea how. Once I was home, and that busy season was finished, I spent the rest of that year taking care of my mom while running a business that was doubling, and then tripling completely out of my control.

I managed to live through a season of my life where my wildest dreams were coming true, while simultaneously waking up every single day to my worst nightmare.

Nothing else in my world could possibly matter, because my mom had stage four cancer.

Throughout that exhausting, impossible time, I learned some things. I did a lot of things the wrong way, and I survived by doing a lot of things the right way. So, my friends, here's what I learned.

Sometimes, you have to force shit.

And for the sake of your dreams, sometimes it is going to feel like the most awful, sick, twisted nightmare, but it is necessary to keep pushing forward when it feels impossible.

Any person who has experienced a huge success in their life will tell you that the Universe has this nauseating way of testing us to see if what we want, is really what we want. When something huge is about to happen for us, BAM – there's the fender bender, or the sick kid, or the lost keys, or the flooded basement, or the crashed computer. It's all a fucking mind game.

The difference between those who actually go after their dreams and succeed and those that don't, is the willingness and fire to push past all of the shit and keep barreling through. Yes, you'll get there all covered in bruises, having not showered in weeks, your sanity hanging on by a thread…

but you'll get there, nonetheless. You pushed through, you forced yourself to just do it even when it was the hardest thing in the world to do. And that's the difference.

Sometimes, forcing shit looks like waking up at the crack of dawn, doing jumping jacks in your living room to wake up enough to get your work done before going to take care of your sick mother. And sometimes, it looks like getting on the damn plane anyway, going to your client and giving them the best business you possibly can, and then letting it all go in the middle of an airport on your way home. Yes, both of these have happened to me. And yes, I am still alive, still standing, still sharing my story in hopes that you will see the light on the other side of the madness.

It is possible to compartmentalize your brain.

Here's the deal, people. Shit happens when you're running a business, chasing after a dream. Your life on the outside doesn't stop just because you need it to. And take it from someone whose business stops when they stop. Sometimes, it's like walking through a blizzard with a little dog who won't potty (if you've been there, oh, how I'm with you).

In order to keep pushing through to the dream, you have to be able to compartmentalize the thoughts that you want to think, and choose to focus on the thoughts you need to think. And this concept takes practice, but the more you do it, the better you get at it. Because it is possible to keep fighting for your dream in the middle of a shit storm. You just need an umbrella and a very large thermos of coffee.

The more you walk through the things that scare you, the hard times that push you, the more incredible the good times feel; the wins, the little victories. And eventually, you'll find yourself accomplishing your craziest dream, a stronger person than you've ever imagined, officially earning your bad ass boss status.

DO WHAT MAKES SENSE TO YOU

Here's the deal. Everyone's situation is so different. For some of you with less stubborn, independent, take-no-shit mothers, that would have been an impossible decision to leave for four months. I get it, we are all walking our own paths, and have to live with our own decisions. And in my case, I was fortunate to spend the rest of that year with her, doing puzzles, talking about news articles and politics, making her lunch, going for walks and laughing about the crazies on the home renovation TV channel (which, by the way, is the most addicting thing on the planet. I highly recommend for a rainy Sunday).

I did what my own situation rendered doable. And there will come a time when you have to do the same—when you will have to make the hard decisions with your back against the wall on the way to your dreams. But in reality, there is no right or wrong. There is only what you think is best for you at the time.

So, by me saying straight up YOU DO YOU, I mean it. You can only force shit and walk through things that truly make sense to force. You can only push yourself to YOUR limits, without sacrificing your sanity, your happiness, your mental/physical health and well-being. But things are going to happen no matter what, and those life-altering moments that the universe puts in front of you are truly, truly made just for your journey.

My favorite quote in the entire world is, "We are all just walking each other home." Everyone has shit. Everyone has burdens on their hearts and stressors that seem unbearable. And one of the things my mom and dad engrained into my brain growing up, was to be kind and respectful and gentle to everyone who walks into your life no matter what, because you just don't know what battles they are fighting.

KEEP FIGHTING

My mother is a fighter and my father is a warrior, a protector. If there is one person who has taught me the vitality of forcing shit, it's him. He is a fierce lover to everyone in his life, and the absolute kindest man on the planet. I've watched throughout my mom's cancer journey as he has stuck by her side, and when the going got tough, he got tougher.

He taught me that there is a certain amount of strength that we all have when we want it, and then a completely separate level of strength when we need it. And we have the opportunity to choose to tap into those separate levels of strength, or let our circumstances eat us alive. He taught me that I am stronger than my circumstances, capable of stepping back, gaining clarity, and fighting on.

What that busy season taught me is that we do not have control over what happens in life, but we do have control over whether or not we will let it define who we are and what we are capable of. I managed to tap into that strength because I gave myself no other option. I put on a face for all of those clients and forced myself to get on plane after plane and fly all across the country to build the company of my dreams, that would years later be more than I could have ever imagined. It taught me HOW to handle anything, and compartmentalize to allow me to control when and where and how I choose to deal with my feelings. It gave me resilience that was impossible to obtain just on my own.

Sometimes it is so necessary to keep fighting, but we have to know our line of surrender. Sometimes, we go through seasons where we can't breathe because life seems so impossible. But the times where we are thriving and living the joy of the reality that we created for ourselves makes it worth it.

I truly hope that you will find release and empathy in this story, and I hope it comes at a time in your life when you need to hear it the most. My story is not an uncommon one, but one that is not brought to surface often. The world needs to start normalizing the struggle, normalizing the hard shit, so that everyone can move through it together, actually believing that it is possible to make it to the other side. Living your dreams will come with more sacrifices and hard decisions than you can count. You just have to remember that everyone is part of the same human experience. You are not alone.

The pain of grief is crippling. As humans, we go through seasons. Dealing with grief as a business owner can feel like a forever winter, a forever season of darkness. And I was stuck in that season for a long, long time, actively grieving while my dreams were happening all around me. It was hard not to resent my business after that summer of leaving. But in the words of my mom: *You have to go through the hard things to become stronger. That's how you learn. The strongest people have endured the most.*

This life is so captivatingly beautiful.

We're all just walking each other home.

CHAPTER 4

Drop Your Fear

What would happen if your biggest fear of starting your business tracked you down and stared you dead in the face? Would you run or would you stand your ground? I'll tell you what I did, because it happened almost instantly after launching. Keep reading.

I am about to get really real with you. I am going to piss you off, and I am going to force you to take a HARD look at how you are living your life. You're not going to like it. But the second I started implementing this concept in my life, it completely changed. And I'm not just talking about a little change. I'm talking fucking massive, mind-blowing change that all these crazies writing books are talking about. So, here it is.

The biggest thing that held me back from achieving my dreams was the fear of what other people might think of me. I played it safe, small, and did only what I knew I could succeed at easily, because I was too scared of going after The Big Shit. I didn't want to fail and be seen walking around with dryer underwear stuck to my pants. (A moment of silence for those who have been there.)

So, I lived for years safe and snuggled in my little bubble, projecting to the world that I was "living my best life" and "making my dreams happen." In reality, I was terrified that I might make a mistake or do something of which people might disapprove or disagree. I was suffocating. I was settling. Hard. But God-forbid I put that out into the world. People might think. . .

I was catering everything in my life to the opinions of others. Yes, I took this big jump and launched a company, and scaled it massively one client at a time, but everything I did after that was based on what others could potentially judge me for. I was worse than a people-pleaser, I was a full-blown life-adapter.

People, please tell me that you hear how crazy that sounds! The life of a people pleaser is no joke. It is hard and frustrating and maddening. A lot of times, you don't even realize you're doing things just to please others. That's the kicker. But so many entrepreneurs and big dreamers get stuck here. Too many start the business or go after the dream and throw it all to the wayside because of OTHER PEOPLE.

I spent years in this space, not giving in to my full potential because of what I thought others MIGHT be thinking about me.

Key word: might

There's a really solid chance that what you think others are thinking is not actually what they are thinking at all...at all! But somehow, those false ideas about what other people think easily build up in your head. Why? Because it's safe.

If you assume people are thinking/saying the worst, you can protect yourself and prepare for when the blow hits. But the critical error happens when the blow never hits, and you've wasted your time waiting. Helmet on, tensed up, afraid to move.

I understand and empathize with this concept: If I think people think I'm going to fail, then I'm going to do everything in my power to play it safe so that I don't fail, even if I don't accomplish the things that I want. That is much easier than actually going for it and failing, to then have to face the fact that they were right about something that they were probably not even thinking in the first place.

In those first few years, I traveled to the care-too-much-about-what-other-people-think-even-though-they're-probably-not-even-thinking-it-in-the-first-place place quickly. Set up camp. Made myself cozy. And didn't dare leave.

But a reality that I found, after years of living in the bad place, is (brace yourself) people do not spend all their free time thinking about your life, because they are thinking about THEIR LIFE. People have way better things to do than sit around all day dreaming up all the instances where you might fail. I guarantee, they're not even paying attention.

So, dear friends, hear me when I say that you cannot live your life that way... in fear, playing it safe, because in reality, nobody actually gives a shit (and I say that in a loving way, of course).

Eventually, you have to make the decision that your dreams are greater than other peoples' opinions, and getting over the fear of that comes from you, and only you, doing an excellent job at managing your thoughts. The second I realized I had total control over the thoughts I have in my head, I started doing bigger things, going for more, taking bigger risks, and seeing the payoff.

And it all started with a few words: *They don't control my life. I do.*

This was my mantra, over and over again, until my stubborn brain hopped onboard with the concept. No, my thoughts didn't switch instantly. It took work. But gradually, the more I used this mantra when my people pleaser came out, the more I took control of my life, the more I stopped playing small.

In year-two of my business, I hosted events, put together

an online resource library, created training courses, spoke at events, and doubled my client load. And looking back on year one, I wasn't ready for any of that. I mentally didn't have my shit together, and physically couldn't take that much on because I was a lost puppy just trying to figure out how to use the calendar app on my phone (it's easy, they said…). And the biggest thing I realized between year one and year two was that climbing from square one up to a massive peak wasn't at all possible with the mindset I had in that first year. It wasn't possible when I gave a shit. And having the big goals that I did, I knew something had to change.

So, I forced it. I made a change. I used the mantra. I fought my inner people pleaser, because I knew the future of my business depended on it. And to be honest, that change was an evil, twisted version of my own living hell, but eventually it became easy, because as I learned in that second year, high volumes of consistent outputs create habits.

Read that last sentence one more time before passing Go.

What would really happen if you just went for it without looking back at the reactions from the crowd? Would your life end if you knew people were judging you? Would you stop breathing if you knew people were talking about you? The ones who say the negative things are the ones who live small lives and could never do what you're doing. They live in a world where their self-esteem increases when they tear other people down. So they talk shit, because that's easier for them than accepting their own life. Negative talk comes from a person's own insecurity and inability or unwillingness to follow their own dreams. It says nothing about you.

Keep that in mind.

Moving on.

You are so much bigger than what other people think of you. You have a light that only you can give to the world, and believing the opinions of others slowly dims your light, until eventually you let it burn out without even realizing it.

The single thing standing in the way of you achieving your dream life is your own damn brain. It's the stories you tell yourself about what others are going to think, or what is going to happen if you go for it. The opinions of others are not what's going to hinder your growth and success in life. No, the only thing that will hinder your growth is how you allow your brain to process the opinions of others.

Allow me to give you an insight into my own crazy brain that first year. I wanted to create an online resource library that would have all kinds of topics in my industry that clients could sift through and find a solution to what they were struggling with. I had so many useful topics I could speak about from my eight years of experience in the industry to share what worked for me, but there was this little (but loud) voice in my head telling me that people would think that everything I had to offer was stupid. They would think that *I* was stupid, that *my company* was stupid, that *my life* was stupid. Yep. Those exact words. Stupid.

"I haven't been in this industry for long enough. I'm no expert…"

Crazy what we can dream up in our heads, right?

I didn't create that resource library the first year because I was scared of what the crowd would say. And it wasn't until the end of that first year when I realized that saying, "Fuck it, I'm doing it anyway." was an option.

That resource library has brought me more clients than anything else in my business. Clients rave about it, because it gives them solutions to problems they have struggled with for a long time. And it wasn't until the first client reached out and validated the library, that I saw any value at all. And once I got that validation (that I soon realized *I never actually needed*), shit exploded, in the best way possible.

You have a choice.

Think of it this way: If you were in a room with everyone insulting you and your work and your life at once, and you had earplugs in, would it matter that they were talking at all? Would it matter what they were saying if you chose not to hear them? You could go on living your dream life with joy and a sexy gumption because it wouldn't matter to you what they were saying when you make a conscious CHOICE to tune them out. You can tell their lips are moving, but you have bigger, badder things to worry about.

It will be hard at first, but put the earplugs in and live your damn life, because I could bet what the crowd is saying about you is not at all what you think it is. I could bet they're talking about what a badass you are, how brave you are, how bold, how good that new dress looks…

You could wait years until you've finally had enough and your life is totally not what you wanted, or you could make that choice today. For myself, I started seeing MASSIVE growth in my business when I finally decided to drop the fear about what other people thought of me. I started doing the big things, the scary dreams, and I did them with my head held higher, and my heart shining brighter. I didn't realize how much energy I was putting toward the wondering, the second guessing, the back-tracking. Once I decided to simply trust myself, everything changed. My life exponentially exploded in the best way possible. And looking back, I didn't need to wait so long. Had I started there, my life would be completely different now.

Don't wait.

And just in case you're the kind of person who needs some tough love: If you're allowing others to decide the outcome of your dreams, then your dreams couldn't have been that important in the first place.

Shall we?

STOP GIVING A DAMN

The dance world is small. Like, really small. Most people know each other, and if not, they have a close connection who does. And on top of that, the dance world is a loyal bunch. I pissed off a lot of people when I first started out. I quit a dance company where I worked for eight years to start a dance company of my own. Although not even close to the same, focusing on completely different aspects, it was a dance company nonetheless. Think of it as an employee of a huge corporate firm quitting to start their own boutique company and taking on clients for one, single, tiny aspect that the firm focused on.

It happens quite often in the business world. But the dance world? That's a unique beast.

Not only did I think those loyal to my former company were all saying awful things; I knew they were saying awful things because they said them…right to my face: "You don't have it in you to be successful. You don't know what it takes. Everyone thinks they can go off and start their own, only to realize later that they made a mistake." Yes, to my face, people. I felt like I was in a shitty workplace drama sitcom.

Besides that, another employee told me, "You don't even want to know what they're *really* saying about you. They're calling you *a snake* and *a bitch* and a terrible person." And no, I didn't ask her. People felt the need to just tell me straight out, because clearly, it was something I wanted to hear… Welcome to the world of toxic women, people. I was surrounded by them, armed with nothing but my morning coffee.

I had prepared myself for this worst-case scenario, except I wasn't actually prepared and would just have to brush these negative comments off. I pretended I was untouchable.

But I wasn't.

On the outside I was hard, strong, capable of being hit. But on the inside, I was angry as hell. Fuming. Constantly. I began to think of those emotions as my norm, as the shell I needed to develop if I was going to make it in the industry. I lost one of my best friends to that anger and resentment. I didn't know how to handle those emotions any differently. It was easiest at the time to just shut the door.

It was like I was self-destructing, while pissing everyone off around me.

Soon after I started my company, my worst fear unfolded, and I had a choice: either run or stand my ground.

One of my first clients pulled me aside before the second day of working with her. Her face was a mix of confusion and right on the verge of pissed off.

"So I got a call today."

I was filled with anger as she told me that she received a call from someone telling her not to work with me. Telling her that I was a terrible person. Telling her that she should find someone else, and even suggesting names of others to work with.

Small, toxic dance world…

I remember my palms sweating and my legs shaking. I couldn't form words. I just stared at my client, trying not to cry. And after I gathered what little piece of human I had left in me, I told her I needed a couple of minutes before we began.

I went to my car and cried. Sobbed. I allowed myself two minutes of breakdown before I turned myself back on again for my client to deliver the service she paid for. Staring at the clock, waiting for the numbers to change, while sobbing uncontrollably for those two minutes was the moment I realized that I needed to rise above. I needed to drop my fear. I needed to stop giving a shit about the noise and start living for me.

I cleared my throat, swallowed hard, and took a massive deep breath while grabbing the door handle. "You can fucking do this" were the words that would decide my future with this company. I would either let the noise shatter me or lift me higher.

I chose the second.

So you want to know if I ran or stood my ground? With fear boiled up to the brim inside me, I planted my feet, puffed up my chest, lifted my chin, and stood my ground with everything I had.

I wasn't running this successful business based on ambition

and hard work. I was running it based on trying to prove that their comments and actions were wrong and that I *was* capable. At the time, I put so much pressure on myself to avoid failure that I lost who I was even before I started. I cared so much about what they thought of me that I went to great lengths to make sure what they were saying wasn't true.

Impostor syndrome hit hard, having the people I once looked up to the most tearing me down, stealing my clients, and saying the worst things anyone has ever said to my face.

I tried to be perfect. I tried to somehow not piss off the people who had already decided they hated me, while continuing to do the thing that pissed them off in the first place.

It was a beautiful disaster of a Catch-22.

Instead of focusing on me and what I needed, I was focused on the biggest uncontrollable in the Universe—what other people were saying about me.

Don't get stuck in that trap. Because truth be told, it's an easy trap to get stuck in. I'm telling you these stories to make you realize that it doesn't fucking matter what noise the crowd is making. It doesn't matter if they're cheering you on with pom poms or openly saying your worst nightmare to your face. It doesn't matter.

Because your dream is worth more than the fleeting words that travel through your ears.

Yes, they might sting—and in some cases, fucking burn—but in the end, they can't touch you. And knowing that, believing that, makes it a lot easier to keep pushing forward. Trust me.

Your worth is much more than their opinions. And it always will be. Your dreams are *your* dreams. Your life is YOUR life. And if you're going after something you really want, something out of the ordinary, something worth fighting for, you are going to piss people off. When you have a dream that is going to better the lives of others and bring a light into the world that doesn't currently exist, pissing the people off who don't understand it and are mad for the wrong reasons is a *good thing*.

And that is one hundred percent the hardest part of starting and scaling a business—doing it no matter what other people think or say about you and your business.

If you are too scared to put your dreams out into the world because of what small people are going to think of you, you are ruining your dream—destroying it to the point of no return. The truth is, if certain people don't support you, and you throw your dreams out into the world and are met with the people in your life making you feel small and insignificant, then those are not your people. Period.

The people who were saying awful things to my face were people who "supported" me for years. They were some of my "best friends," and at the time when our dreams aligned, they truly were. But when I decided my dreams were different than theirs, that's when their true colors came out.

Never change your dreams because of the people around you. Instead, consider changing the people around you because of your dreams. You will find that the people who are meant to be in your life, meant to follow along with you, will support the crazy. They will support the messy journey, the long nights, the rain checks on coffee, because they will understand the vitality of taking action toward what you truly want in life.

Other people are not allowed to dictate your life. It's time you made the conscious decision to move forward from that.

TAKE WHAT IS YOURS

You want to do big things? You want to move mountains? You want to go after the SUPER dreams? Then you cannot give a shit. Plain and simple. You cannot care how you are rolling in to the coffee shop to get your caffeine fix (in my case it's usually in my pajamas from the night before) or how you sing and dance in your car because it fuels your joy (using my coffee as a microphone) or how you talk to your dog like a person because you work from home (because they're your real ride or die).

If you want your life to be yours, then you have to take it. You have to put your ear plugs in, drown out the noise of small peoples' opinions, and do it for YOU.

If you never make that decision, no one else ever will.

DROP YOUR FEAR

Your ability to decide to go after your dreams despite the fear of the outside world will be the first step in your journey toward the mountain. In fact, it might just be the thing that gets you halfway to the top in an elevator.

I had to stop listening or the noise would destroy me. And for a while, it did.

Because the shit no one tells you is that pretending not to care and actually not caring are two completely different things.

So, take baby steps. And take them one day at a time. Situation by situation.

It'll be gradual and it'll take some patience and perseverance, as this is something that doesn't happen overnight. I NEVER believed that I was capable of doing this. And for me, it took a lot of tender, loving care (and a bit of elbow grease). But know that is normal. It is human to not like it when someone talks behind your back. It is human to care what others think of what you are doing with your life. And it is human to cave in to those emotions time and time again. But if you want your dream, and I mean *really* want it, you have to put your ear plugs in, be aware of when you're caving to the outside noise, and then shut that puppy down.

Because your dreams are worth it. Your future is worth it. The hardest part is the first step.

Cheers to your dream. It's happening.

CHAPTER 5

Have a Thing

*I*t is so easy for a new, inexperienced entrepreneur to get swept away with it all. The building, learning, working, pushing…it's enough to make you lose your shit. And year two, I lost mine. Completely. However, it wasn't because I was working so hard (but maybe, kind of, a little that). I lost my shit because I wasn't doing anything to take care of myself. I wasn't giving myself breaks, indulging in things that made me happy, or taking the time to stop thinking about work, even just for a second.

The loss of control came when I completely neglected myself, putting work above absolutely everything else. So, let's deep dive into this mistake, shall we? Buckle up, people.

I developed adult acne at the age of twenty-five. And no, not just a few pimples, but an insane number of red dots covering my entire face (I know…but I promised I would get real. Stay with me here.) Now, if you have not faced the Everest that is adult acne, I'm going to let you in on the madness. It is just short of wanting to jump into the deep end. Terrible.

I was embarrassed to talk to people. I felt dirty, disgusting, ugly. I was crawling in my own skin, itching to get out, but there was no way out. I was stuck in a face with little red dots covering the whole thing.

I felt powerless.

The worst part about my acne at that time was that I was "just too busy" to actually address what was going on. I used products that burned the shit out of my face in hopes that if I put my face through enough, then my acne would wave the white flag. But it didn't happen quite that easily.

I ended up caving and seeing an acne specialist. I was on a seven-step regimen, but still the little red dots found me. It felt like the more the acne creeped in, the more stressed I became thinking about it. It was to the point where makeup wasn't even worth it. The acne destroyed my self-esteem, one day at a time. It made me depressed, frustrated, and constantly paranoid.

If you've been there, you get it. This shit is no joke. And if not, you lucky ducky, hang in. I have a point.

I found out after three years of dealing with the beast that it was all a reaction to my stress (and sugar… People, candy is not the answer. As a desk candy snack person, I'm right there with you. Hold strong). The times I was most stressed, the little red dots came out to play. It was to a point where I knew I had no other option. I had to chill the hell out. My lifestyle was affecting my body. A change was necessary.

Side note: This took me three years. Do NOT let it take you that long. If something is wrong with your body, figure out what might be causing it internally. Take a long, hard look, and then take action. Because you do not need to live this way, in tolerance.

So, after a few books, a come-to-Jesus meeting with my acne specialist, and a total mental breakdown, I decided to get real with my stress. Nip it in the bud. Throughout the next few months, I learned some stuff that changed my life. Naturally, we're going to share that next. The things that are so necessary to staying sane, satisfied, and stable. The shit no one told me.

Say it with me: Self-care.

In other words, the biggest loaded word in the world. The shit no one told me.

I really hate to be the one to break this to you (although, I hope I'm not the first), but most of what you read/hear/ingest is total bullshit. There are a million articles out there that will tell you exactly how to do it, what to buy, how long to do it for, how often to do it, and where to go to get the coolest and most expensive/effective shit you need to take care of your inner self.

So, I'm going to be real with you all and let you in on the secret that I've found to real self-care.

There is no secret.

Self-care can be anything you want it to be. Yes, anything. If taking the baths and getting the massages and listening to the music does it for you, fabulous. If dancing around your house with your dog in hand and singing old-school Taylor Swift does the trick, then that is all you need. And yes, that is very much something I do regularly. My dog loves it.

The mistake people make in glorifying self-care is that they don't put enough emphasis on the "care" aspect of it. Everyone is so different. What works for you might not work for other people. And that is okay. Do what brings you joy and calms the stress. Because what some people are doing nowadays for self-care would NOT work for me. For example, the candles and face masks—can't do them. The essential oils and yoga—hate them. They make me MORE anxious than when I started.

Side note: My absolute favorite (and by favorite, I mean most self-explanatory, straightforward, yet highly underutilized) advice I've ever read about self-care—use your sick leave. People, if you're not using your sick leave at work, we need to have a chat. Because that time is YOURS. This is your permission.

Moving on.

Self-care is supposed to be a judgment-free zone, but instead, society has made it this glorified social media concept, making it necessary to get the perfect picture of your bubble bath; otherwise it didn't happen. Well, let me tell you, you can sit in a bubble bath all day long, with the froufrou candles, expensive bath salts, oils, and the "ocean waves" playlist on your speaker. But if you get out of that bath and go back to being the same exact stress ball you were when you hopped in, then we didn't fix any problems, my friend. We just put them on pause for a hot second. And not only did you just waste your time, but you added that much more built-up stress into the picture. What's the point of all that?

The beauty of self-care is that you can use it to EVALUATE your life. You can use it to look at how you've been handling the bullshit and make actual change to fix the maniac that you've become, running into traffic and cutting your bangs. Self-care is a time for reflection, a time to create space for yourself in a world that is constantly telling you that you are not enough. It is a time to stick it to the madness and show up for yourself as someone who is taking control, commanding your own life.

In Minneapolis, we have this thing called "Top the Tater." It is a glorious concoction of sour cream, chives, and magic. My self-care nights consist of sitting down with a full bag of regular potato chips and a tub of "Top the Tater." Yes, most times I finish the whole bag. And yes, all the times I enjoy it. No guilt. That is my indulgence, and to me, a huge form of self-care. Why? Because it forces me to stop, breathe, enjoy, and get back into a clear head space. Now, I'm sure there are healthier ways to accomplish it, but this is my thing.

The reality is, your self-care can look like anything you want it to. If it helps you chill the hell out, and STAY THERE, then it can be whatever you want. But the trick is using your self-care for good and inner improvement, not pretty pictures for social media and a check on your to-do list. The results come when we do the thing and then say, "Okay, now what?" When we use self-care as a tool to get better, it is then serving a purpose in our lives, as opposed to a Band-Aid over a gaping wound.

It is all about finding your release, and whatever helps you do that, then by all means. Because the fewer crazy zombie humans we can have running around, the easier it is to go to the grocery store without wanting to tug on the ponytail of the lady in front of you taking her sweet time at the checkout.

The trick is to do self-care before you reach the point of really NEEDING self-care.

THE TRUTH ABOUT BURNOUT

And with that, let's talk burnout for a second. My "dream job" consisted of me traveling all over the country whenever a client wanted me to. I had no structure, no balance, and I said yes to EVERYTHING. Now, don't get me wrong. Over the years I developed a structure to my schedule and started saying no to the things that didn't make sense for me at the time, but I was still trying to do everything at once. And of course, I was invincible (no one could tell me otherwise). Oh, to be young and naïve.

I didn't only think, but I *believed* with every ounce of my being that I was the only person on the planet who could do what I was doing. And if you've been there, you know how easy it is to get stuck in that trap. I thought that clients would drop me if I couldn't make the date work that *they* wanted, dropping everything else in my life. And along the way, in the midst of it all, I lost myself.

If you don't have a stubborn personality, first—bless you. Second, allow me to fill you in. I literally ran myself dry for years. YEARS. I was doing every single thing that anyone asked of me, half of the time not even charging my worth, and going, going, going until I was falling asleep at the wheel, or needed the flight attendants to wake me up once we got to the destination. "Yes, I'll fly across the country to meet with you for two hours…and yes, I'll do it for half the price because it's not in your budget for this year… and of course, I'll make the five-hour drive to work with you because you booked last minute and a flight was super expensive…and yes, I'll work for nine hours straight with no break so we can make the most of our time together."

The filter system in my head, the one that was supposed to

allow me to say no, the one that was supposed to control just how crazy my life became, was broken.

I was screwed.

But I was the one who broke it. And although I knew how to fix it and I knew why it was broken in the first place, I couldn't bring myself to get my shit together. The next client was too important…

My lack of boundaries caused my burnout.

My diet consisted of fast food on the road, ginormous glasses of wine when I finished a job, and very little water. I didn't sleep because I was too anxious about the things I had to get done. Most of the time I sacrificed sleep altogether so I could get things done and the stress would subside for a hot second, until the next thing.

I was a MESS. My body hated me. I had constant headaches, acne that was out of control, zero natural energy, and I promised myself I wouldn't let my mother read how much caffeine I was ingesting—so you don't get to read that one—and I always felt like shit, nauseated and overworked. But naïve, stubborn Marissa wouldn't slow down for half a second to figure out the little things that could make her not feel like shit. I was twenty-five years old and knew every single thing I needed to do to take care of myself, yet I just wasn't doing it. Soon after, I found out that doing self-care was an active *choice*. But believe it or not, in the moment I didn't see it as such.

It is easy to get swept away with it all. Life has a funny way with that. So, in order to avoid getting swept, you need to make the time to get your shit together. You need to schedule in that time to chill. For years, I thought that everything I was doing was way too important to stop and take care of myself. I didn't realize that if I would have just stopped to take a break, I could have propelled forward at twice the speed.

The shit no one tells you.

You need to stop for gas in order to get to your destination. You cannot keep plowing through on empty and expect your car to arrive magically. Because if you do that, you'll find yourself stranded on the side of the road, quickly running out of snacks.

Self-care doesn't need to be these big events that take hours and hours. They can be minutes of singing to your favorite song in the car, drinking a yummy coffee, or smelling the flowers on your way into work. I believe these moments are what create sanity. I'm not one for huge gestures, just little things to prove to yourself that you deserve more.

And sometimes, that gesture needs to be saying no.

JUST SAY NO

We cannot dictate the direction of our lives based on the needs of other people. Being a "yes" person is not serving anyone. It is only causing pain. And you may not see it right away, but it will surface. Trust me on that. You have to take care of yourself. Figuring out how much you can handle has a learning curve. The trick is to figure it out quickly, and make your decisions based on that amount.

Stop doing the shit that you can't actually handle. Your sanity is everything. In case you needed a little permission, there you have it. You CAN say no to things and still be a beautiful, gorgeous, worthy human. It is necessary.

The path to living your dreams will require you to work harder than you ever thought you would need to. Yet, you will get there faster if you allow yourself time and space to unwind.

I spent *years* so focused on the growth of my company that I neglected everything and everyone around me.

We called them family dinners, my friends and I. We would get together for dinner and then grab drinks out on the town and talk about life and laugh and dance and just enjoy each other's company. It was a pretty regular thing for a while, usually every other week or so, and I would wake up the next morning feeling loved. And honestly, there isn't any other way to describe it. Those dinners, those nights with the people in my life I cherished the most, made such an impact on the way I saw the world. I valued that time, more so than just about anything else.

And then, one day, I had to say no. I had a client book, and I was so excited to grow my client base, I said, "Sorry, but next time." And just like that, it all started.

Golden Shit

The first no was easy. I was excited for the new client and the chance to grow my business. But the second, third, tenth time, it got a hell of a lot harder. Each time was more painful than the last, but the little person inside of my head (although at the time growing bigger and bigger by the second) wanted me to grow my business. And the obsessive person that I am, I listened.

As good friends do, they called me on my shit. They pleaded with me to take a night off and come back to the family dinner for just one weekend. Well, this wouldn't be my golden shit if I didn't royally mess up here.

You guessed it… I didn't go to that dinner. I spent that evening with a client and didn't look back. And after that weekend, I stopped hearing from them.

Two weeks later, when I expected to get a message chatting about the details of where to meet that evening, my phone was silent all day. And that feeling of impact, of love, took a hard 180-degree turn.

I felt a pain that I still wrestle with occasionally, because going through that was not easy. And what I didn't realize at the time was those dinners were what saved me. They were what kept me grounded. By neglecting them, I was really just neglecting myself and what I needed to feel happy and loved. Welcome to another one of my major screw-ups.

I just "didn't have the time" to commit to social things, which I continued to tell myself until it became my story.

Work is important on the way to your dream life. But so is sanity. So, if that morning coffee with your girlfriend or that workout session with your gym buddy or that family dinner with friends who you consider an actual family is calling to you, answer the damn phone.

There will always be more clients. Don't make the same mistake I did.

Just say no.

THE MESS OF TOO MUCH

Okay, I'm just going to say it straight out, and some of you are going to get your undies in a bunch, but here it is. There *is* such a thing as too much self-care.

Society has normalized the phrase so damn much that some people are walking around doing constant self-care, not doing anything that is uncomfortable, skipping work, and allowing their version of the phrase to completely ruin their lives. Quitting your job because your boss wants you to work on a project that is going to require you to stay an extra hour every evening for a week IS NOT SELF-CARE. It is NOT setting healthy boundaries. It is entitlement and pain-in-the-assery.

The phrase is so normalized and "trendy" as a constant reminder to do the things that serve you, to actually force yourself to take breaks when you need them before you crash and burn. It didn't used to be so normal to take time for yourself. People used to work to the bone until they were practically passing out taking their kids to soccer practice. They would work seventy-hour weeks, and after getting home from a long day, help their kids with homework, fix dinner, and get about four hours of sleep before doing it all again the next day. And THAT was normal. That was my parents, God bless them.

But here it is, the shit no one tells you.

It will be like that at first. You will work your ass off, do things you don't want to do, and constantly have your brain running on overdrive, because when you're first starting out, the good shit is flowing. The creative ideas, the excitement, the energy, it is all there. And the beautiful thing about the normalizing of self-care is that you know you need to take those breaks amidst all of the good shit. You can still work seventy-hour weeks when you are first starting out, but at the same time, know (and EXECUTE) what you need to stay grounded. So many people know the validity of taking care of themselves, and what will happen if they don't, yet they don't take action. Don't be that person.

Take breaks as you see fit (there is no right or wrong), and show the world that you are the badass boss of your own life.

Balance, people. Find yours.

Period.

THERE WILL ALWAYS BE SOMETHING

The first year in my business, I had a four-hour drive home from a client. I knew all day that I wasn't drinking enough water, and I could feel it as the day went on. Now, if I had a desk job, this would not be the end of the world. But my job is to essentially WORK OUT for the entire time I am with a client. I am on my feet, moving, teaching, dancing, jumping, sweating, and being in four places at once—watching every detail and sprinting around to see it all from every angle. When I am with a client, I am dialed in with every single ounce of life in me. Well, ten hours later, when I finished with the client, I hopped right into my car and started driving so I could get home as fast as possible to get the most sleep that I could for the next full day with clients.

About an hour into the drive, I found myself on the side of the road, puking from exhaustion and dehydration. Alone on an interstate. With zero help.

Looking back, I'm still not sure how I made it home. Shaky, lightheaded, nauseated. But throughout that whole day, I knew this would be the result if I didn't drink enough water. I felt my body reaching its max, but I still pushed through, not taking the two minutes to rest and drink a little water.

I crashed and burned. Learn from this, people.

In those first few crucial years, working will be everything. But don't let that be the reason you are puking on the side of the road because you didn't make pit stops along the way.

You WILL get to your dreams. But don't be in such a hurry that you forget to fuel your engine.

The fact that self-care is now a highly talked-about, normalized concept is something we should be very thankful for. I don't know about your parents, but my parents taught me that when we are very thankful for something, we don't abuse it.

So, here it is. The simplest, yet totally underutilized concept in the world: Work your ass off for what you want, and take time to smell the roses.

Slow down when you feel that stress ball forming and know when it's necessary to keep pushing a little further to achieve what you want. Because, straight up, building my niche company to that level in three years all by myself was hard fucking work. Most of the nights that I worked until the crack of dawn were completely necessary. But, instead of enjoying the time I had off with the loves in my life, I was stressing about the next thing and doing busywork. I needed that time off with those loves, yet I believed I had things that were more important. Looking back, I needed to be doing self-care to get my shit back together before moving forward. And I would have gotten to where I was a lot faster if I had allowed myself that time.

The hardest thing about chasing your dreams is the feeling of guilt for taking time off in your business. I get it. At the time, it always seems impossible, because there are ALWAYS going to be things… Always.

HAVE A THING

There will always be something to work on, dreams to chase, and money to make. But there are only so many beautiful moments with the people and things you love that you'll never know existed until you lean into them.

Will sings to the dog; he is that type of person. One who makes you feel comfortable and loved.

He also cooks every Sunday night. He enjoys it because it helps him combat the "Sunday Scaries"—that feeling on Sunday night when the anxiety and anticipation about the week ahead overpower your ability to be a normal human.

I used to work every single Sunday night until bedtime. I would come home to Will already in bed and my mouth salivating from the yummy smell of whatever he cooked for dinner. I would take the leftovers out of the fridge, heat them up, and eat dinner by myself while trying to combat my own Sunday Scaries.

One Sunday, I randomly had the night off, which was a rare thing at the time. I came home at about four o'clock on a crisp fall day to the smell of a delicious dinner seeping through the open windows to the front steps before I walked in the door. I saw Will in the kitchen, multitasking with different pots and pans, and our dog at his feet waiting patiently for dropped nuggets of food (he always gets something, whether we try to drop it or not). As I walked into the kitchen, his smile radiated. He greeted me with a kiss and a steaming bite of chicken fresh from the pan.

When I dropped my things off in the bedroom and changed into my comfies, I felt something that I hadn't felt since starting my business.

I felt home.

If there is one thing I actually regret in those first few years, it is not allowing myself those Sunday evenings more. Because all of the clients, all of the hours spent working will never amount to the feeling that overcame me that night. The feeling that growth in my business could never give me.

The feeling of coming back on Sunday nights to dinner cooked, a clean house, dog toys scattered on the floor after a long day of playing, and Will holding the dog with one hand—singing and softly bouncing him while stirring the noodles.

The feeling of pausing. The feeling of being in the moment. The feeling of enjoying the little things. The feeling of actual self-care.

Don't let that next thing, that next dream, that next idea be what hinders you from actually enjoying your life. I'll let that marinate.

You find LIFE in the slow moments. Those are when the biggest epiphanies and crazy ideas come knocking. But if you are too busy working, you won't hear them at the door.

I came up with the idea for this book while looking out the window of an airplane above the clouds.

I pieced together the idea for my company while sitting on a beach in Florida.

And I created the business plan that doubled my client base while brushing my teeth, after snuggling on the couch, in my fuzzy socks, with a cup of hot chocolate, watching a Christmas movie.

We are all so different. And the beauty of it all is that you can experiment to figure out what works for you and how often you need it, before becoming a crazy zombie woman.

Whatever your release—be it sex, a bubble bath, a bag of chips and dip, a froufrou face mask that cost you more than your last grocery run, or a Sunday evening dinner with your hubby—just do it when you need, how often you need, without judgment. And when you get really good at this whole self-care thing, you'll learn to listen to your body enough that you'll know when you need it before you actually need it. Hence, saving your love life, not scaring the dog, and protecting the world from the mess and a half that is you experiencing burnout.

Stop the madness. Stop the guilt.

You deserve self-care. You are worthy of taking the time to take care of yourself. Just because you haven't "made it" yet doesn't mean that you can't take a break. I guarantee you won't even come within arm's reach of "making it" if you don't.

You'll be too tired to care.

This life was made for you, the big things, and even more so, the little things.

CHAPTER 6

Perfect Is Fucked

Welcome to an entire chapter dedicated to the fucked-up reality of "perfect".

Let's start from the beginning.

I had this need since I was little to be perfect. I grew up dancing in a pre-professional dance studio. I trained thirty-hour weeks before I hit middle school. Dance was my addiction. It was my obsession. And I truly loved every second of it.

Every day, my mom would pick me up from school and drive me to the studio, where I would spend six to seven hours training. When class was finished, my dad would pick me up and drive me home, where I managed to quickly (and half-assed) finish my homework before heading to bed.

I never realized it at the time, but I was always sleep deprived, always exhausted, never slept more than six hours a night my entire childhood, and I had zero true friends outside of the other dancers that I trained with.

But at the time, none of that even registered with me, because I so badly wanted to do it all. It was my passion, and I was truly in love. Lacing up my point shoes gave me life. I felt like I truly had a purpose, that I was working toward something, improving, climbing.

Dancing made me feel vibrant. And I will never be able to put that feeling truly into words, but it was everything to me. My whole life revolved around it. And I wouldn't have had it any other way.

Growing up, I also had the need to be good at anything and everything that I touched. And training to be a perfect little ballerina managed to fuel that need…a LOT. The truth is, I was good at training. It was something I worked my ass off for, but I always seemed to have the competitive edge, the ability to read people and read situations to figure out how to get ahead, paired with the drive and work ethic to make it happen.

In high school, I got all the awards. I was captain/leader/ president of so many things, which allowed me to be in every social circle, because that aspect came naturally to me. I was self-labeled as the overachiever. I knew what I wanted for my future, and I knew that those things would help get me there.

College was easy for me, as I picked majors that clicked, Communications: Leadership & Advocacy, and English. I read two books a week, wrote papers on papers, and learned how to communicate effectively in different settings. I was thriving. It all came easily because it *was* easy—as it was all my strengths combined. I actually looked forward to going to class and doing the work outside of class. My future just seemed to fall more and more into place every day.

Being a perfectionist who was good at the things with which I surrounded myself, I developed these expectations that my whole life would be like that. I had incredibly high expectations because I had accomplished what I thought were huge things—and had to overcome very few obstacles to get there.

Therapy, people. Don't think for a second I realized this all on my own.

Fast-forward to when I started my business, and my world came crashing down around me. The perfectionist who needed everything to be by her standards, who had always picked things in her life that were connected to what she was good at, was now standing in a flooding boat, trying to scoop out the water with a bucket the size of a shot glass. Constantly.

So, I stopped eating.

Yes, you read that right. I developed a wicked eating disorder that controlled my life. It started out small, as a way to feel like I had a grip on my own reality. And then it fucking exploded.

At the start of my second year in business, my clothes no longer fit. Everything was baggy, and I just didn't care about my appearance anymore. Every day, I wore sweatpants that fell off my body, had stomachaches that consumed my mind, and was repulsed by the feeling of being full.

But the messed-up part? It felt good to do. It felt like I was finally in control of my life and making progress. I knew damn well what I was doing, but I couldn't stop, because I finally felt sane. I finally felt free.

I remember going a whole day without eating. All I had was my morning coffee and water. During that day, I also crushed in my business. I accomplished a few really big goals, and I attributed that to the control I had over everything (not the massive number of inputs I was making in my business).

Another day, I returned from two weeks straight of traveling with back-to-back clients. I sat on the couch next to Will, and he pushed up the sleeve of my T-shirt and brought his hand to my upper arm. His fingers touched as he wrapped them all the way around it, grabbing nothing but bone. I looked up at him to see tears in his eyes. It completely broke my heart. I knew I was hurting him. But I couldn't stop. I couldn't get my shit together. *I didn't know how.* So, nothing changed.

Strike one of 253.

I kept at it, the barely eating thing. And when I did eat, I felt like a total disaster, a failure. Not because I ate, but because I lost control.

I was not starving myself to be thin. I was starving myself to prove that I was in control over my wild, messy life. I had created a six-figure business in two months, and I didn't feel like I'd accomplished anything. Why?

Because it wasn't how I pictured. It was messy. Awkward. Scrappy. Imperfect. Therefore, I couldn't grasp it as my own definition of success.

I had insane expectations as to how every single step in the process would go. I had everything planned out as a perfect little picture in my head.

Until not one single thing went according to plan.

The clients were rolling in, but not how I thought they would. I was working from home, setting my own schedule, but not how I thought I should. I was working my ass off, but not how I thought I could. It was all happening, but it was beyond imperfect.

I was trapped between my need for control and the lack thereof. Because as an entrepreneur, there will always be things that you want to control but never can. It is fleeting, heavy. And if you let it trap you, that feeling is almost impossible to escape.

Learn from this shit.

In the case that no one tells you, allow me. When pursuing your dream, more times than not you feel like a failure, a total catastrophe. You can be doing everything right, and it can still feel that way.

But hear me when I say that none of that is attributed to your success. It is one hundred percent attributed to everything happening in the most insane way that it possibly can, and looking the polar opposite of what you thought it would.

But nonetheless, *happening*.

The friendliest reminder to you all. You do NOT have control in your business, and it will NOT be perfect. You cannot control whether clients screw you over, or if something massive fails that you saw through to the bitter end. But you CAN control how you handle everything. You can control your emergency plans, your backups to your backups. You can control the work you put in beforehand, and how everything is handled on your end.

And you can let go.

Let go of your expectation of the how, and start focusing on the what. On the end goal. And KNOW it is FACT that nothing will go down in the pretty, perfect, picturesque, champagne-toasts-on-a-gorgeous-boat-watching-the-sunset way that you think it will.

Story time: I booked an Ivy League school—yes, a REAL IVY LEAGUE—as my first major client. It was my first year owning my business, and I booked A FREAKING IVY LEAGUE SCHOOL. ME! A NOBODY. BOOKED AN IVY LEAGUE SCHOOL!

In case you were wondering my exact reaction when it happened.

I worked my ass off, cold-calling clients and reaching out to people who had no idea who I was, trying to sound like I hadn't been stalking them for quite a while. And after a few months of that madness, I got a call from them asking if they could hire me. Of course, I said yes, trying to remember to keep breathing on the phone and act even slightly chill. Which, looking back, I am so sure I didn't.

We solidified the details and I was off to the races, booking my flight and hotel, which ended up being just under $1,000. At that time, $1,000 was a shit ton of money (I think if you have student loan debt of any kind, any amount of money is a shit ton of money to you). But I knew I was going to earn that money back in less than a month. So, I ripped off the Band-Aid and booked.

Two days before I was headed out there to work with them, I got a cryptic voicemail saying they would no longer need my services. No explanation, just a straight-up "Thanks, but no thanks."

Have you ever seen the movie scene where the actress stares out of her cab window in the rain, crying silently, feeling sorry for her existence? That was me.

For a month.

You guys. It was bad. It was my first let-down. My first screw-up. And the first time (sadly, not the last time) I failed to take responsibility for my actions. "How could this possibly be my fault? Nothing bad could ever happen to me. I am just starting out! This was supposed to be easy! No one told me that this could happen. I wasn't prepared!"

You want to talk crazy train? I was the freaking conductor, as that was my exact dialogue for way longer than I would like to admit.

Because on top of that, I didn't get reimbursed for my booked travel. And that, at the time, was quite possibly a million times worse than losing the Ivy League client. It was the first loss in my business, which is, without a doubt, the hardest loss.

I blamed the whole world. I felt like a complete failure. I was out $1,000 that I would never see. I was just starting out and had no freaking clue what I was doing, and I just lost a major client that would have been my big break into the Ivy Leagues. Instead of learning from the experience and moving past it, I let it destroy every ounce of self-worth I had.

Even that *failure* didn't go the way I expected. It wasn't all perfect.

The shit that no one tells you: Your success in your dream amounts to your level of self-worth and respect. If you let it.

As a new business owner chasing a big dream, I believed that. Wholeheartedly. And I let my perception of the success of my business dictate my entire life.

It took me WAY too long to realize losing that client was the best thing that could have happened in my business. It taught me to check my shit. It taught me to slow down and be more detailed. It taught me to be more even-keeled and not put so much weight on my wins and losses. It taught me that I am more than my success, that I am more than the perfection in my business.

What nobody tells you when you're venturing off to take the jump toward your dreams, all bright-eyed and bushy tailed, is that nothing will work out the way you thought it would. You don't have control, and having expectations will be the cause of your need to take sleeping pills just so you can calm the hell down at night.

But the messed-up thing was that it was decently easy to see success in my business quickly, even though absolutely nothing was even close to my standards of the way I wanted it. Booking clients and growing my base was easy because I picked something that I was good at, something I could get excited about. It was easy because I was in my bubble of everything I thought, at the time, could be perfect.

I was seeing success, but I wasn't actually *seeing* it. The rest of the world was seeing it and then telling me about it. "Wow, you really are living out your dream life." "You are radiating success!" "You turned your dream into a job! How incredible!" "The level of success you've had in such short amount of time is so inspiring…" Those are the comments I heard constantly. So, at that point, I felt like an outsider to my own life. It was like I was living my life but was so removed that I couldn't feel anything.

I was numb to my very existence.

CUT THE EXPECTATIONS

The constant stress that you feel, even though you are seeing actual success, is the Universe hitting you with a two-by-four. When you feel that stress, one of two things is happening: Either something is not happening within your own parameters of perfect, within your pretty expectations, or the thing that is happening is not actually the thing that should be happening.

The truth is, it shouldn't be perfect. Perfect is safe. Perfect is boring. Perfect is small.

Perfect is fucked.

The single trap that is going to cause your demise in chasing your dreams is having hard-set expectations, not only about what you're doing, but about where you are headed. NOTHING will happen the way you think it will. And God Bless America if we are too stubborn to think otherwise. Take it from a person who had to learn all of this the hard way.

Chill.

BE A BADASS

The thing is, it WILL happen. You are the badass in control of your dreams. You are in control of the work you put in. And you are in control of whether or not you let the little details of The How impact your pride and enjoyment of everything finally falling into place with The What.

I needed to experience what I did as a business owner to report back to the masses all of my epic mistakes. I needed to walk directly through the shit to discover my true path. And if I had continued grasping on so tightly to my own definition of perfect, I never would have seen my true purpose coming out of the woodwork.

You might have this vision in your head of what it's really going to be like—following your dreams. And the real magic doesn't happen until you lose that vision and open yourself up to what is calling you, what excites you, and then follow that. The path to your dreams appears when you step out of your own way. Then, and only then, can you experience what you're truly meant to do.

LET GO OF THE STORY

Stressed, worried, anxious, and gripping tight because of the fear of the unknown? Let's remedy that, shall we?

Allow me to take you back to when I first had the idea that I wanted to start my own company.

I planned out EVERYTHING. Every single detail that I possibly could (or better yet, thought I should). I planned out my days as going to the local coffee shop, listening to my podcasts on the way to the co-working space where I had a membership, before heading home to dinner with my loving husband and a relaxing night at home. I planned on spending our weekends traveling the country and exploring the city where we live, spending time with family and friends, filled with nothing but joy and gratitude for my beautiful life.

Guys, my first move as a little premature business owner was to buy a cute picture frame for my office. Oh, how times have changed.

My issue with this day-to-day plan was that I was dead set on it all happening just as I had pictured it. In reality, I would spend the next three years straight after the launch with zero weekends off, almost zero nights home for dinner with my handsome-as-hell husband, Will, losing my love for sitting at coffee shops and a million other small things in life I once loved.

So, here I am, telling you how it is. Again, you're welcome.

The road to your dream life is not sexy. And it will NOT follow most of the steps of your game plan. It will NOT be perfect. But that is freaking normal!

I let fear get in the way of my progress. I clung on with a death grip to a reality that didn't exist. I was scared of failure. The more things didn't go as I had planned, the more I held on to the things I had left that could go as planned. But I learned some things throughout that process, and having a clear picture in my head wasn't the issue—holding onto it was.

So, here's what I have for you to fight the fear, fight the perfect expectations, and make shit happen.

Every single day, take actual physical steps toward your dreams. They can be teeny tiny steps, but those are steps nonetheless. Make those phone calls, send those emails, create those imperfect ads, go to town with a plethora of content that you only 90 percent approve of, and EMBRACE THE IMPERFECTION OF IT ALL. Because if you're like me, it will never be as perfect as you want it, and the sooner you can move on from that mindset and just fucking do it anyway, the sooner you get to that dream life.

BE FLEXIBLE

You're going to have a list of things you want to accomplish. And then you won't accomplish them. You will have things that you accomplish that you never thought you would. Life is filled with so many twists, you can't possibly predict where it's going to take you next. So, my advice? Set goals that you want to accomplish, and then see where those take you. One at a time.

Be flexible in the twists and turns and your day-to-day operations at the motherboard. The How doesn't matter. The What is what you're after.

But the "I want to start the business of my dreams by twenty-four, be married by twenty-five, have a baby by twenty-seven, my last baby by thirty, become a millionaire by thirty-two, and a multimillionaire by thirty-three" has GOT to go. The Universe has a better plan than you could possibly dream up on your own. But the dreaming helps with your ambition, and your ambition helps with the action to get there.

I NEVER pictured myself here. Writing this book. To the masses. Exposing my biggest fuck-ups.

Never.

Trust me, what I had planned was a lot more modest and cute than this. But life threw me over the edge. It tested me in a way I never thought I would be tested, and it left me with a decision to make: continue to grasp on until I stopped breathing, or follow where the Universe is telling me feels right.

I chose the second.

FAILURE IS WHAT YOU ARE AFTER

Sometimes it doesn't work out. Sometimes you see very little progress when you've been a flying crazy monkey and let your life fall to shambles because you've been so focused on work. But that is GOOD! Let me tell you why.

Failure is either a loss or a gain of momentum. And you have a choice of which one it is going to be for you. You can let failure destroy you, or you can let it be the driving factor behind actually achieving your dream life.

My advice: fail hard, let it soak in, take a shower, and then get pissed as hell as you plan your attack. Because the payback you get on your failure could be what completely rocks your world.

Read that four times before moving forward.

People, I was a hot mess. I failed more times than I can possibly count, all for the greater good of the cause. But of course I didn't see it like that at the time. There were more times than I would like to admit where failure completely destroyed me. It wasn't only a loss of momentum, but a grinding halt altogether.

Throughout those losses, I learned what it meant to trust the path. I learned what it meant to choose to keep walking. And I learned that a grinding halt doesn't have to be forever.

You get to decide.

GET BACK UP

I woke up one morning in my hotel room after a ten-hour, exhausting, mental-capping day before with a client. I was dehydrated, sore, nauseated, and still in my clothes from the day before. I went to the sink to wash my face and placed my hands on the edge to stabilize my dizzy self.

Tears welled up in my already swollen eyes as I stared at my face in the mirror, a face I no longer recognized. My cheekbones were sticking out, my skin was pale, dry, and filled with acne, my lips were cracked, my hair had thinned out, and my teeth were bright yellow.

I no longer recognized myself. I was disgusted.

I stood there and cried for as long as my eyes produced tears, and then some time after. I allowed myself to feel the grief of letting my perfectionism destroy me, to feel the weight that I created myself. I knew this was my fault, and I knew I needed to fix it.

Slowly, I turned the water on, grabbed my face wash, and bent down to wash off all of the things that disgusted me about my reality.

And then, I fucking got back up.

The most important thing you can do to show up in the world is continue to get back up. Every single day. And yes, sweatpants are socially acceptable for this event.

I wish I could fully explain it for all of you out there just starting out, but this is something you have to feel on your own. There will be so many times when your emotions toward your dream change. One day you will wake up and feel absolutely unstoppable and want to take everything to the next level, times a million (it could be the espresso, but we take what we can get…). And the next, you'll want to burn that shit to the ground. This is such a real thing.

When your dreams are truly big enough, you'll constantly teeter the line of fucking unstoppable and all sanity lost. But if you go into it knowing that this is going to happen, the whole process is WAY easier because you can then accept what is happening as a normal step in the crazy process.

The thing is, no one told me that it was going to be like this. I thought I was going to wake up every single day and be so obsessed with my company and the work I was doing that I couldn't even stand it. Little did I know…

Everything you had planned on the way to your dream, that beautiful, perfect journey you've always pictured, will be ridiculously imperfect. There will be disappointment, messy times, full-blown arguments with the Universe. But I promise, the sooner you accept this, embrace it, and find joy in it, the more you can love the process.

Don't miss your dreams unfolding in front of you because you're stuck in the details of how it happened. Because it WILL happen, and you're one step closer now.

You got this, fighter.

CHAPTER 7

Control the Energy

I didn't buy into the energy, voodoo shit for years. I always (internally of course because god forbid I piss someone off) rolled my eyes whenever someone talked about energy. But a not-so-quick spout of depression, total indifference to life, extreme anxiety, and enough burnout to completely extinguish the fire in me completely changed that…on the whole energy thing, oh, and the ability to piss people off without giving a shit.

Picture this: I am in my first year of running my choreography business, all twenty-two years of life in me. Everything is great, or so it seems. It all felt damn good at the time and it was exhilarating and fun and ego-boosting.

I was chasing after every new client, every sale, every traveling opportunity, and of course, making everything public so I could show the world all of the excitement in my life. I was saying yes to EVERYTHING, to every single client who wanted my services, including the ones who couldn't afford me (but I did it anyway and charged way less if I had the date free... That's a discussion for a different time). I was spending hours and hours traveling all across the country to be there for what seemed like a few minutes, before traveling again to the next client.

My social media feed read like a highlight reel of a baby goat on cocaine. I was smiling for the camera, looking all cute, jumping around, and chasing my tail like crazy, so excited to be alive.

Or so it seemed.

But as my busy season subsided, and I had literally eight months of downtime, everything came down crashing and burning and then was shoveled up, stuck in a sewage waste pit, ground up into a million pieces, and served as my morning coffee.

I couldn't get out of bed. I couldn't laugh. I couldn't breathe. I hated everything and everyone. Life made me so fucking angry, and I couldn't explain why. I put Will through a living hell. But he was the only one. Because on the outside, I was living my best life, and to the rest of the world, I was on fire, unstoppable, and so damn happy.

While on the inside, I was dying.

I remember freaking out one morning because my shampoo was almost out and it was tricky to squeeze the last bit out of the bottle. You guys, I actually screamed at the bottle. I flipped the flip out and threw it on the floor of the shower and started crying. Crying because I couldn't get the shampoo out of the bottle.

And while I would love to tell you that was indeed my breaking point, my actual wake-the-fuck-up moment didn't come until about a year later.

My stress, anxiety, and depression were all getting gradually worse throughout that year. I had developed acne so bad that I had to see a specialist, not for adolescent acne, or even adult acne, but for *stress* acne. I had gotten to a point where I legit couldn't handle anything. My shirt had a wrinkle and I would flip out. My coffee was a bit too cold and I would lose my shit. And you don't want to know what would happen when actual things that meant something would go down. I was Britney Spears circa 2007. And if you need that explained to you, well, that makes me feel old. Look it up.

I was wound so tight and three inches away from losing the love of my life. (God bless Will. No words...) My family should have hated me (but they're all kick-ass, epic humans, and I got lucky in that department). And I had managed to push every single friend out of my life who ever meant anything to me. I was straight out of control.

It wasn't until Will and I hit our breaking point, the

something-needs-to-change-or-we're-done breaking point, that I woke up to it all.

Will: "Marissa, something needs to change."

Marissa: *aggressive exhale

Will: "I'm so sick of where we are and how you've changed and I want to fix it."

Marissa: *silence

Will: "We need to talk about this. I can't keep doing this."

Marissa: ...

After a six-hour conversation of this, a six-hour conversation of Will being brutally honest and me sitting there just taking it straight, we aired it out. We didn't fix it, that came sometime later, but after that talk, everything was on the table. Now he had permission to call me on my shit the second I became a cranky gremlin.

Now we were making progress.

It was not until that point that I realized I was being reactionary about everything in my life. I had zero control over who I was and what was happening inside my mind. I never stopped to take control of the stories I was telling myself and the reasons I was feeling certain emotions. I was just allowing the outside world to dictate my life.

So, here's what I have for you. Let's learn from my mistakes, shall we?

You have COMPLETE control over one single thing in your life: your mindset. And whether or not you decide to manage and take control of it will be the deciding factor for the life you will live. Managing the thoughts that go into your head, the thoughts you allow yourself to process, defines who you are and what you do with your life.

For years, I did not know how to manage my mind. I had no quality control center in my brain telling me that the thoughts I manifested and the stories I was telling myself about my toxic actions or unjustifiable inactions were complete bullshit.

"I'll never get more clients. I peaked early and anyone who would ever want to hire me already has."

"I shouldn't have started this in the first place. I don't know the first thing about growing a business. I am not smart enough for this."

"Who am I to be marketing ANY of my services. I am not even close to as good as that girl. I am not enough to keep going."

"I am trapped in a financial reality that is dependent on me working non-stop and traveling constantly. I can't get out, or else I'll be seen as a failure."

"Who am I to take a day off? I am not even close to where I want to be. I don't deserve it."

"This is hell."

I had no barricade, no security screening with plastic bins and metal detectors and people walking around with no shoes on. I was so easily influenced by anything that entered my brain.

Until someone told me I had a choice.

Naturally, I didn't believe the concept was that easy at first. It took a while of trial and error, as I was stubbornly set in my ways, but the minute I started actually trying to filter my thoughts, everything changed.

And not in a small way.

YOU GET TO DECIDE

The wild thing about life is that you decide the energy that defines you. You decide to take the thoughts that enter your mind as gold, or throw them out completely. You are the *only* person who is making up stories in your head about your own reality and why you can or can't do something.

For me, I flipped the script. It was the hardest thing I have EVER done, took constant work, and yes, I failed at it. A lot. But the more I did it, the closer I inched to the healthy mindset I practice today.

"I'll never get more clients. I peaked early and anyone who would ever want to hire me already has."

Then becomes: *Clients love your work and you will continue to grow your base one client at a time, just like how you started. There are so many clients out there, and they are slowly finding out about you. Keep doing what you are doing. It's working. Stay the course.*

"I shouldn't have started this in the first place. I don't know the first thing about growing a business. I am not smart enough for this."

Then becomes: *Starting this business has made you a stronger woman. Yes, it is hard. But you can do hard things. You've already established that. And you know who can pull off doing the hard things over and over? Smart people.*

"Who am I to be marketing ANY of my services. I am not even close to as good as that girl. I am not enough to keep going."

Then becomes: *Every single person starts somewhere. There is no magic button. Put in the work and you can get there. And get your ass off of social media because that is ruining your healthy mindset and you get stuck in comparison mode.*

"I am trapped in a financial reality that is dependent on me working non-stop and traveling constantly. I can't get out, or else I'll be seen as a failure."

Then becomes: *You have the ability to hire a team. You have the ability to say no when you know you will face burnout. You can travel smarter, take days off, and fuel your self-care needs to make you stronger and more capable of doing the crazy busy season.*

"Who am I to take a day off? I am not even close to where I want to be. I don't deserve it."

Then becomes: *If you don't take a day off, everything is going to crumble around you. You have let this happen to your life before. You are allowed to take a day off. You are not a robot. And doing so always makes you more productive anyway.*

"This is hell."

Then becomes: *Yes, this is hard. But there are so many things over which you have control. Let's visit some of those, shall we?*

Like I said, this shit is hard. But the more you practice, the more repetition, the better you get at it.

This changed everything. Every. Single. Thing.

And yes, you just have to force it. There is not an easy way to do this, and I think that's the bullshit that society has allowed to become normalized that is causing so many mental health issues as a result of negative self-talk. Positive mental talk is fucking hard. And that is straight fact. But it DOES get easier the more you muddle through it imperfectly.

THE ENERGY DEFINES YOU

The energy you ingest and the energy that you give out to the world completely define who you are. Therefore, you have to protect that shit like nothing else. You cannot allow the comment your mother-in-law made, the jerk who cut you off in traffic, the negative review from your boss, or the look your dog gave you define how you are going to live your life. And when you're feeling the weight of the world around you, the heaviness of comparison, get off of social media IMMEDIATELY. Just put the phone down and get your ass outside for a walk.

Your circumstances do NOT define you. How you respond and react to them does. How you process them in your brain does. How you live your life in the moments after does.

Protect your energy. And pay attention to it. Years, people. That's how long I let my energy define me. For some people, it's a lifetime.

You are the only person in control of that.

THE REAL SHIT

All throughout my experience with depression and burnout and too much anxiety and stress to physically handle, the one thing that would have saved me from it all, avoiding MANY nights of wallowing and lost sleep and bad decisions, was knowing how to handle my emotions.

It is so important that we feel. It is so important that we do not internalize emotions until we are bursting. It is normal to be sad or mad or angry or stressed. It is all part of the human experience to feel those things. The danger comes when we allow ourselves to feel it, but then we don't have a healthy way of moving forward.

The danger comes when we don't do what we need to manage our own mental health.

Making the decision to get help was the hardest thing I have ever done. I still remember how I was shaking when I made the call. Like, what do you say in that situation? I didn't know. I think I stumbled around with, "Hi, um, I am looking to talk to someone. I have stress, and um, I own a business, and I, ah, found your info online, and um…" Pretty sure that's when words stopped forming altogether. Cross "good when nervous" off my list of emergency skills…

But I can't stress enough how important it is that, as business owners and entrepreneurs, we get rid of the stigma of seeking help.

Figuring out the "business" side of a small business is NOT the hardest part in starting a business. The hardest part is the emotional side, the mental side, the side that forces you to deal with all of these factors that you weren't prepared for when you first started out, that you had no idea were coming, but that are now literally slapping you across the face, over and over again.

Finding the clients, structuring the business, setting up a financial tracking system, creating ads, pushing out content, client communications, and scaling were *not* what knocked me on my ass. What knocked me on my ass was dealing with my limiting beliefs, dealing with my stress, my anxiety, dealing with the story I convinced myself in the beginning as to why I wasn't worthy to have the business of my dreams—the story that sunk in and stayed there.

These are the things that no one is talking about. The real kickers. And it's time. It's time we talked about these issues and brought a light to a topic that is sheltered from the world really seeing its true face.

Glorifying entrepreneurship is the cause of so many mental health issues.

The fucked-up part?

NO ONE IS TALKING ABOUT IT!

Entrepreneurs first starting out see the glamour. They see the wealth and the big houses and the nice cars and the fancy clothes and the cocktails on the rooftop and the lavish beach vacations. They don't see the shit.

So, what are new entrepreneurs grasping onto when they get into their business? The comparison factor. They're grasping onto what they're seeing on the outside from those who have gone before them. The belief that things should be different, better, easier, putting an unrealistic end goal on a pedestal. And what is the cause of all of these mental health problems in entrepreneurs? The social stigma surrounding it all.

It is HARD working alone. It is lonely as hell, maddening at times. I was always so jealous of the companies who have a whole team at the office every day. People to talk to. People to bounce ideas off of. People to not make you feel alone. And think working from home is lonely? Try traveling the country alone for four months straight. That really fucks with you good.

It is HARD not knowing when that next client is going to come rolling in. There were so many seasons in my business when I was scared. Scared of when I would get paid again, scared that I wouldn't be able to scale again, scared because I would see the mountain ahead and knew what I would have to go through to reach it. Scared when I was so far in student loan debt, among other things, and the sole thing pulling me out was the work I was putting into my business.

It is HARD scaling and not having a single clue what you are doing. Most days, I would wake up and wonder if what I was doing was even making an impact at all. And most days I convinced myself that it wasn't, that what I was doing was a waste of time. I felt worthless. A fraud. Incapable.

It is HARD showing up day after day when you are un-motivated. When I was first starting out, that motivation was coming from me, and only me. And that might have been the hardest part (there were a lot of hardest parts…), motivating myself when there was no one else to cheer me on.

It is HARD to face the crowd when you don't want to do the madness anymore. And for so many entrepreneurs who decide that this life isn't for them, they're faced with the perception of failure from those around them. The perception of failure from themselves. And that is terrifying.

It is hard.

We need to be sharing what it's actually like at times to be an entrepreneur. Of course we also need to be sharing the successes. I am absolutely going to tell you about all the trips I took this year with my husband, and how I finally paid off my student loans, and how we got the house of our dreams, and how we're shopping for condos in paradise. But I'm also going to tell you the shit that I went through to get there. Because we cannot be glorifying entrepreneurship without sharing the other side.

We need to start normalizing talking about this topic because it is so damn important. The people entering into this realm need to be prepared so that they can take precautions and prevent a lot of this from happening. But if we only share the good things, the brag-worthy things, then we are doing a disservice to society, to our fellow entrepreneurs.

Breathing life into a company for the first time, being there for all of its successes, all of its failures, building it up, investing so much time and energy, tweaking every little detail so that it's perfect and everything you wanted…it's petrifying.

We cannot let this slip.

Every decision you make is all on you. Your mental health is the most important thing. The only thing. And you have to get it in check because your entire life depends on it. You have to make decisions that are going to support your well-being. And you have to cut out the things that don't.

Talking to someone is what saved me. Hiring a life coach to get my shit in order and bust through mental blocks is what saved me (she is the real MVP). Seeking guidance through meditation and healing energy is what saved me. There is absolutely NOTHING wrong with doing what YOU need to get healthy. Because what worked for me might not work for you, and that is okay.

THE GAME CHANGERS

How you respond to the world around you is 100 percent your decision. Do not let your past, trauma, and years of believing the beautifully told lies tell you otherwise.

I once blew up at an airline agent when my flight got cancelled. And blew up as in actually blew up. Bad. I was stuck in Austin, Texas, and had to cancel a client and a shoot and a personal commitment the day after because I couldn't get home. Instead of making light of the situation and choosing to see how another day in Austin, just relaxing and exploring, wasn't actually a bad thing, I chose to see the negative. And I chose to let that negative ruin the rest of my trip.

I could have chosen to be chill to this agent on the other line, as the flight was cancelled because of bad weather—really nothing he could control at all—but instead, I decided to destroy his day and fly off the handle.

"You just don't get it... Let me speak to your manager... You're not hearing me, I NEED TO GET HOME... Like, this is your job, isn't it?"

The second I got off the phone, I took a step back in utter shock. Was that really me on the phone? Did I actually just yell at a random human trying to do the best they could? I was ashamed. And ashamed is my LEAST favorite feeling, if there was one I had to choose never to feel. I acted out of character.

I watched as my life collapsed around me in slow motion from the weight of my own stress. I walked the streets of Austin, bawling, heels in hand, mascara running down my face, ugly, ugly crying. That was the final straw. Until that moment, I didn't see it. I was completely blind, consumed by it all.

Because that's how it happens, little by little, until there's no other option but to break.

I couldn't handle even the smallest thing going wrong, because I refused to take control over my mindset. It just seemed simpler the other way.

You don't have to let the stress in little by little. You don't have to allow yourself to reach the point of no return. You have the choice, and the second you realize that, and I mean *really* let it sink in, the sooner you can filter out the bad shit and live the extravagant life you were meant to live.

And if I can do it with my life literally in shambles, so can you. It is an easy decision, but a strategic practice. Not difficult…strategic. Here's what I did.

How to chill, lesson #1: Get to know what sets you off

Date it. Meet the parents. Put it in a box. And throw that shit away.

Okay, people. This is a no-judgment zone (in case your brain is currently telling you otherwise). That means a no-judgment zone for YOURSELF. Yes, that includes you, Sparky. No exceptions. Because you are about to bring shit to the surface that you would never want exposed. The shit that you've been internalizing and burying for years.

This is the shit that only happens behind closed doors: the yelling in traffic, the cursing at your computer, the throwing of your phone, the pounding on the desk, the chest tightening from anxiety, the heavy sighs at night on your pillow. All of it.

And with that, we're going to expose WHY those things are happening and what triggers them. Most of the time, those triggers are sneaky little buggers who slide by without you even knowing it.

The shit that you bury is down there for a reason. There could be a million different reasons, but you decided to internalize it because of *something*. For me, it was fear that I was a total fraud, that I wasn't good enough, smart enough—that I was going to fail. I was twenty-two years young after all (back when I thought that mattered). So, instead of bringing that to light and dealing with the mess, I dug a hole, threw it down there, filled it in, and built a house on top of it.

The thing that killed me slowly was neglecting to realize that truth. I wasn't awake. I wasn't *paying attention*.

People, when you constantly feel like you are about to break, are triggered by every little thing, and can no longer handle things that used to be no big deal, WAKE UP. Do not let it consume your life. Take control. Leave little reminders around your life to pay attention to what sets you off, and then deep dive into why that is happening. And yes, this is as simple as asking yourself, "What in the actual hell am I freaking out for?"

But then you have to answer that question.

That's the hard part. That's the part that may leave you feeling icky. But trust me, it's worth facing the icky, so as to avoid the catastrophic devastation that comes when you don't.

You react to everything in your life for a reason. And those reactions are valid. They are human. But when that human starts to turn into a crazy monster with green hair who destroys cities, it's time to take a step back. And yes, you're allowed to have a glass of wine during this step in the process. That's normal too.

How to chill, lesson #2: Take a long, hard, brutal look at the story you're telling yourself.

This one's my favorite. There is a HUGE difference between what we perceive as reality and what actually *is* reality. And most of us are quite skilled at convincing ourselves of pretty much anything. So, as per my promise, here's the shit that I did.

I am only twenty-two. I know absolutely nothing about business. I have zero credibility or way of getting credibility. There is no way I am going to scale this. I am not smart enough to pull this off. Anything that happens from here is dumb luck. I am going to fail.

This is the story I told myself every single day. And I got so good at telling the story, I completely convinced myself that it was true, to the point where I began self-sabotaging myself and my business to prove the story correct.

Building to the level I did in two months should have been a huge accomplishment. But it wasn't part of my story. My story was to fail. Therefore, I allowed myself to feel like a total failure because I wasn't proving my own made-up story correct. I had the successful business of my dreams, yet I couldn't enjoy any of it. I couldn't believe any of it because I had done such a good job at convincing myself that the lies were truth.

Do NOT perfect your own messed-up narrative to the point where you actually believe it. Yes, doubting is normal. But catch yourself in the act before it's too late. Allow those thoughts in, and then push them out just as fast. Don't let them sit there and set up camp.

I catch myself in the act when bizarre limiting beliefs pop into my head, and then ask my brain very loudly, *BUT WHY?!* Why are you thinking like that when there is no proof?! Why are you blindly following the thoughts that clearly need to pack their bags and get the hell out? A thought is simply that, a thought. It holds no weight. And it surely doesn't have any control over you because you are capable of changing that thought using the same device that put it there in the first place: your brain.

Your real story deserves your full attention.

How to chill, lesson #3: Protect your house.

You cannot let just anyone wander through your wide-open front door, go into your fridge, and eat all of your string cheese without your permission. You have to protect your string cheese. You have to shut your front door. Not lock it. Shut it.

I'm talking about setting boundaries, protecting your energy.

If you allow the outside world to burn down your house, then you will have no house. If you allow others to steal your joy, steal your energy, then you will have none left for yourself and for the things and people you truly care about.

I let clients walk all over me. I let toxic friends make me feel guilty for growing my business. I let people gossip, spread drama, infuse negative into my life. Constantly. So, when it came to my family, Will, my true friends, I felt like I had nothing left. I was empty.

Now, as a human, you should not lock your door and hide the key. You are not allowed to go into hiding and not let anything in. (Been there. Done that. Five years later and here we are.) You need to learn from your experiences, not use them as ammo in a war waged against yourself and the world.

Life is meant to give you joy, not to take it away.

But there will be times when you come across people and experiences that test that notion, try to break through your boundaries to steal your energy. And that is what you need to prepare for, what you need to protect. You are allowed to cut people out who destroy your happy, and you should. It really is that simple.

Whenever I felt the most overwhelmed, it was because I was not setting clear boundaries. Technology has the world feeling like we are all on everyone else's time frame because it is easier than ever to communicate instantly. The issue is the underlying pressure of feeling like you have to *respond* instantly. It's time you set boundaries in your life so you are not readily available all the time. Allow me to share a couple of ways I do that myself.

Number one: I do not open or respond to texts (unless it is from my family or husband) until I know I have the time to respond. This is a game changer, people. I found that my brain was going in a million different directions, constantly, because I was opening and reading and responding to every single text I received, the second I received it. Therefore, my emotions were at the mercy of the buzz from my phone. Lesson learned the hard way.

Number two: I turned off my email notification on my phone. YOU GUYS. This may seem like a simple little thing, and I know you feel like you need to be available for every single email the second it comes in, but this system works for me, especially in times when I need to be the most creative. So, instead of checking my email multiple times every hour whenever a message comes through, I check it five times a day. No, I am not saying you need to take it to the max and check it only once per day. You can still stay on top of your email without responding to each one right as it comes in. Yes, yes, you can.

If it is not serving you, not growing you, not bringing you joy, keep your front door shut. You don't have to share your string cheese if you don't want to. It's your choice.

COMMAND YOUR OWN DAMN LIFE

In order to get to where you want to go, in order to move those mountains, you have to control where your energy is placed. You have to live with intention and purpose. You have to be a master of your own mind. You have to take control of the things you allow to come flying out of your mouth and the things you allow your brain to process as truth.

Your dream is happening. Treat it as such.

CHAPTER 8

Get Yourself Some Systems

I was driving from Milwaukee to Minneapolis after spending a couple of days with a client. As per my normal five-hour drives, I stopped for some road snacks before heading out. (I always get gas in the morning on the way to my client, and snacks on the way home. I get the boring thing that I don't want to do out of the way first, and the exciting thing comes as a reward after I finish a job. Would it be more efficient to do it all at once? Yes, yes, it would. But I live for the little treats in life, and my brain is funky, as we've established.) Placing my Cheetos and jerky on the checkout counter, I pulled out my wallet to pay. After scanning my card, in the kindest tone, the man behind the counter said, "I'm sorry, miss, but it looks like your card was declined. Do you have another one?"

My heart stopped. Because I didn't have another card. I had my business debit card, the card I always used on the road, the card that was locked from my savings account, the only funds I had available to get me to Minneapolis. Five hours… on one tank of gas.

I apologized for not having another card, left my snacks at the counter, and walked to my car, nearly in tears.

Starting my car, I looked at the gas meter, and thankfully, it was full (my ritual paid off that day). I had one tank of gas to get me home. I had more miles to go than the amount that was in my tank. So, I had no other choice.

I started driving.

I pulled up my maps app so I could keep track of the miles I had left, drove in the slow lane the entire way, and went fifty miles per hour in a seventy zone THE ENTIRE WAY HOME (to get the best gas mileage… I don't know, I read it somewhere once).

Five hours later, exhausted from the energy I was expending looking at my miles, my tank level, stressing the hell out, and holding in my urge to go to the bathroom, I made it home. With two miles to spare.

You guys, I didn't have money for gas because I forgot to pay myself before I left for the trip. I didn't have a system for paying myself in MY OWN FREAKING BUSINESS! Me, the business owner. Somehow running a multi-six-figure business, but she couldn't remember to pay herself.

GET YOURSELF SOME SYSTEMS

You ready for some truth?

First, let's talk systems before moving forward. A system is something in your business that sets you up for success in an organized, get-your-shit-together kind of way. Every business needs different systems, but regardless of what you choose for your system, it keeps you intact, keeps everything flowing smoothly, keeps your ducks in a row, keeps you from freaking the hell out at a gas station in Milwaukee.

The first year in my business, I thought I was invincible. I thought I knew everything about everything and could manage every single aspect of my baby business on my own. Well, clients came pouring in, and I had no cork to stop the water, no strainer to filter it through. I was stranded on an island that I had created for myself, every day getting closer and closer to pure insanity.

I had over 2,000 emails in my inbox that were not organized (yes, you read that right), invoices strewn about on my desk, a piece of notebook paper to track my finances, and a solid chance that I didn't set my business up correctly through the state. But I was WAY too busy to handle all of that. After all, I had a business to run, clients to book, places to go.

I was in straight denial of everything happening within the walls of my little home office. I continued to tell myself that I would take a day to "organize" and "regroup" after the busy season subsided. Because that's what normal people do, right? Take days off?

Well, not me. I enjoyed teetering on the line of no return, apparently. And the part that screwed me and this mentality I had set for myself? My busy season never subsided; it just got busier.

So, I continued on with the madness. I allowed my inbox to pile up to 9,000 unfiltered emails that first year, I somehow tracked my entire stream of income on notebook paper, and I managed to run my business structure on an ever-growing to-do list.

Well, eventually, as you can imagine, this all caught up to me.

When I missed a client.

I got the call about ten minutes after the start time, with the client frantically asking if everything was okay. I remember the shock that ran all the way down to my fingertips, and stayed there, as I drove very much over the speed limit to get there for the final half hour of time. I made no excuse. I just sat there and took it. I told the client this slipped through the cracks, and it was a huge mistake. I was mortified. How could I have missed a client?! I had a *system*.

I went back over emails, and there it was. I had all the information. I just neglected to put it in my calendar.

And in case you're wondering, I did not let myself live this down for longer than I would like to admit.

Forever thankful to the business gods for gracious, understanding, kick-ass clients…

You guys. My system broke down. Hard.

So, that next month, I did not pass Go. I did not collect $200. I got my shit in order, instead. The client flow was not steady that month, but I regained my sanity, and my business.

I set up a system for my emails, a system for my marketing, a system for travel days, a system for organizing finances, and a system for tracking the client process. These systems were all what made the most sense to me. Nothing fancy. I didn't go the "popular" route with what I was using if it made me feel clueless and lost. I didn't buy the shiny programs or the complex software. I chose the systems that clicked with *my* business, during my busy season and my still-busy-but-not-as-busy season.

See, what no one tells you when you're first starting out is that your business, your dream, will go in waves. There will be months when you feel on top of the world, organized as hell, and then there will be months where everything crumbles in slow-motion right before your eyes. And sometimes, it goes from one extreme to another in a matter of four seconds. But you can semi-avoid that crumbling, or keep it from happening in slow-motion, if you set up intentional systems that keep things flowing smoothly.

These systems do not need to be perfect or glamorous or

anything that you would ever put on social media, but they do need to exist to some degree. And the truth is, there is no right or wrong way of setting up your system. I never got rid of my ever-growing to-do list. I just changed the structure of it. I never organized the inside of my inbox. I just developed a way of never missing client details through a process that I am pretty damn proud of.

There are so many "experts" out there, quick to tell you that your system is incorrect, and that only certain things work if you truly want to be successful. But I promised to tell the truth to you all, so allow me to call bullshit on the experts.

I developed a system that works for me, one that probably makes others cringe. And I have seen others' systems that have me reaching for an afternoon margarita, but totally works for them. I have scaled a business using to-do lists and a messy (but organized, like how I leave my clothes on the floor) system that makes sense to me and how I operate. If someone were to make me put all my emails into little folders, and number my to-do list by priority, and time out my coffee runs in my calendar, I would lose it. Because that just doesn't work for me and how my brain operates—and there's a chance it never will.

Just because your system is different from the norm doesn't mean it is ineffective. Yes, the guy next door might be kicking ass with his online fitness business planning sheet, but that doesn't mean you need a planning sheet for your dream. Have I banged this on the head hard enough yet?

YOU DO YOU, BOSS.

Period.

DETERMINE YOUR END GOAL

The biggest thing I did for my business when I was first starting out was find out what I needed, and then get creative on how to execute it based on a system that worked for me. You cannot have a system without an end goal. The end goal dictates the system that you create.

If I were a florist, my process would look polar opposite. Same for an engineer, a graphic designer, a full-time mom who does ALL the things. Structure your day-to-day based on what your goals are, what you want to see in revenue, client count, accomplishments for the month and year. Each month, your system might look different, and that is a GOOD THING. That means you are catering to fit the dream, not catering the dream to fit your systems. Because if you do the latter, it's harder to get to the champagne pop. Not impossible, but harder. Don't repeat my mistake, people.

Get your ducks in a row. Spend some time with those ducks. And then move the ducks around how you see fit.

The closer you get to your dream, the more you will want to tweak your system for the current step you're taking. By all means, tweak. Because every single step of the process will look different.

Once I decided to get my shit in order, my systems changed about every couple of weeks. I don't believe that one size fits every situation. Nor do I believe in keeping a process for the sake of staying the course, when you know there is a better way that will work for you. The more I learned about business, the better I got at filtering out what no longer served the process to my end goal.

The #1 rule in chasing your dreams: There are no rules.

Find what works for you and continue to adjust. There will never be a perfect system, but you do need to have one. Something. Making mistakes due to your own stubbornness is not an option for you, sir. You have too much potential, too much drive, too much dream.

Coffee. Desk snacks. Systems.

CHAPTER 9

Screw the Stress

Welcome to the mistake that changed it all. The mistake that I struggled with the most for the longest time, but finally figured it out. The mistake that saved my life, baby step by baby step. The mistake that is inevitable. The mistake I wish I had been prepared for... Let's start from the top.

I was a worrywart. I worried about the past and things I couldn't fix or change but wanted so desperately to fix or change that I would worry about scenarios that could never come true; they already happened and I couldn't do anything about it. I worried about the present, every single moment of the day—how the details of my day would pan out, making sure everything was going according to plan. And I worried about things in the future I didn't even have fully planned out, ideas that weren't fully ready to execute, wild scenarios that were straight impossible, but I allowed myself to worry about the "what if's" in the rare case that they were possible.

I was a fucking nightmare. Relaxing and enjoying the moment was a far-fetched concept. I couldn't shut my brain off. I jumped from one scenario to the next so fast that I would heat up my coffee in the microwave after letting it sit for too long, wait too long again to drink it because I was distracted by my own thoughts, only to repeat the same process four times before finally taking a sip and then setting it down to forget about it again. Any microwave coffee people out there?

I was grasping so tightly to my business and my life that worrying somehow made it easier to cope with a future that was so unknown. I would let thoughts control my brain constantly, and I wasn't able to enjoy (or process, for that matter) the moment, ever—I couldn't remember details, events, things I needed to take care of, because I was so caught up in jumping to the next thing, worrying about whatever I could in my business.

Present in the moment was a far-off concept, a unicorn idea that couldn't possibly be a reality for business owners and big dream chasers.

The shit no one tells you.

I was in a sick cycle of trying to control everything before it happened, and somehow stressing about those things made them easier to control. When you're in it, and I mean *really* in it, what you are doing in your business feels like the most important thing in the entire world. It feels like the only thing. And of course, no one can understand it because you're the only one who is capable of grasping the concept of your business and what you are going through, right?

Wrong.

But I'll cut you some slack, because it does feel like that when you're first starting out. There is nothing wrong with feeling like your business is the end all, be all of the Universe…but just for a little bit. Then it's time to let the green monster go back into the box.

Anxiety and stress have a way of rearing their ugly heads into your world, only to create more anxiety and stress because you're anxious and stressed about the anxiety and stress you had in the first place.

Am I making you stressed? Keep reading.

I allowed anxiety to take over my life—always thinking about the next idea, the next thing I had to worry about—because I couldn't get a grip on my own reality. I couldn't stay present in the moment because of all the things I had built up in my head regarding scenarios in the future. Truthfully, it sucked. It was an awful way to live. And it made me neglect things in my life that could have made it all go away. Have you ever heard of a bull head? Yes, hi. That would be me.

So, people, I am going to deep dive into what I did to change all of this, what I did to stop the madness and pull my shit together. Get a refill on your coffee, tea, blue slushie (no judgment here), and let's begin.

Ways to not let stress ruin your life:

#1: Focus on what you *can* control, and kick ass at that.

The only thing I could control in my business was my output. I could control the number of potential clients I reached out to daily, what my process looked like, and how I showed up for those clients who did sign on.

So, every day in my business for that first year, I reached out to at least twenty new clients in some way. I knew that those initial interactions were crucial, and I tailored every message to each individual client. I did my research. I put in the time. I wasn't just trying to sell a product that I could throw in clients' faces a few times with basic marketing. I was selling *me*. They needed to know there was a person on the other end, a person who cared.

After I signed a client on, I made sure that process was absolutely seamless. I had a calendar of scheduled touch points before the date of service, templates, phone calls set, the whole shebang. I wanted this process to be refreshing, one they had never gotten from a choreographer before. And I knew I was in control of every step of the way.

Throughout your journey, there will be a lot of things that you cannot control. Those are the things you will want to stress the most about, because as much as you want to do something about it, you have no power over the situation. Therefore, it is WAY easy to stress. And that is quite the kicker.

But you will also have a lot of things you can control throughout the journey, things you can get really stinking good at, things that—when executed correctly—change everything. Those are the things to focus on because you can actually make an impact. You need to choose to kick ass at the things you have power over, the situations that can make waves in your success outcome.

There are going to be WAY more things that you cannot control than things that you can. But the key is getting really good at identifying the things in both scenarios, and then taking action toward them to decrease the green stress monster.

For example, playing every single scenario in your head as to whether the client on the other end of the ringing phone is going to chew your head off for calling them? That would fall into the can't control category. But being prepared for your pitch presentation so you don't put your foot too far into your mouth, that would fall into the can control category. Do you see the difference? Kicking ass at preparing for your pitch will do WONDERS to decrease your stress level.

So, choose to do that instead of replaying the failure that hasn't even happened, and probably won't, because you're a fearless rock star.

The second you choose to kick ass at the things you can control is the second that everything changes. You become an unstoppable machine, a business superhero, a fucking genius. Because that choice is the hardest one to make on the way to your dreams. Too many let the uncontrollables take charge, instead of taking charge themselves toward the controllables.

#2: Find a thing that will reel you back in to reality.

I use sticky notes to remind me that I am a human who does NOT get to become a monster because of the path I chose. I use sticky notes to remind me that the shit isn't really that bad, and my stressing about the shit only multiplies the shit. I use sticky notes in every single room in the house so as to not fall into the deep end with the stress and anxiety and sharks and slimy fish.

"Yes, you fucking can."
"Strive satisfied."
"Show up consistently."
"You are smart AND you are capable."
"You are greatly influenced by your words."
"Switch the laundry…" (because we all need a little bit of that energy in our lives).

Sticky notes are my thing. They are what reel me back,

constantly. I use them to remind myself that there is SO much more to life than the stress I have created. Let me repeat that for my friends in the back…the stress that I HAVE CREATED. Because that's all this is, right?

Stress is beyond easy to create, and if you get really good at creating it like I did, you will find yourself running the streets with a bag of chips and a hammer (because destroying your life one step at a time makes you hungry for snacks).

So, in order to avoid all of that, you must have a thing that is going to reel you back in. It can be simple, like sticky notes around your house or a desktop screensaver, or it can be big like a tattoo across your forehead. You do you, ma'am. No judgment here.

It is so easy to get caught up in it all when you're working for yourself, when your own actions, and your actions alone, dictate your success. I never felt this way in the corporate world because I had a team of people who I could fall back on, a team of people to lift me up when things went south or I was having a bad day. But when it's all on you, you have to do the things that are going to help take the weight off. You have to learn to *manage* the stress so you can stand in the light and be happy. Because that is a thing, you know. And it is possible.

Having a thing to reel you back in to the reality that you are living helps with the craziness of it all. It helps keep you grounded, and reminds you that although you are stepping toward your dream life, you are also *living* the process to get there—which is way more important.

#3: Find your exit buddy.

I have multiple exit buddies…multiple people with whom I share the weight of my dreams. Because sometimes, your dreams are heavy. And sometimes, one person is just not enough to help you carry them. So, I don't have one buddy. I have people. To name a few…

One is a photographer. She and her husband travel the world and photograph weddings and engagements and other larger-than-life events.

Another is a choir director, pianist, and overall magician, transforming mediocre musicians into world-class artists.

Another is a stay-at-home mom. She manages her family and the rest of the Universe. Her job is harder than most.

These are just a few of the people who hold me up when I am collapsing from the weight, bring me back to reality when I have strayed too far into crazy land, and listen when my mouth becomes uncontrollable—spewing out hopes and dreams and fears and worries and overwhelm and evil green monster.

These people keep me connected to my dreams. They remind me why I started in the first place whenever I want to throw in the towel; they keep me trucking when I am on a momentum high; and they slow me down when I have turned into a wrecking ball, chasing the next dream before the oven timer went off on the last one. My exit buddies kick ass. And the best thing they have ever done for me was refuse to no longer be one.

You guys. I was a terror. For years I refused to take control over the things that were ejected out of my mouth. I was passively living my real life, and actively living in my business. So, with everything that related to work? I was a rock star. But with everything that related to my personal life and actually being a good human to the people I love? I was AWFUL. I acted as though I didn't have to take responsibility for the way I was treating everyone around me because I was chasing my dream, after all. Nothing else could possibly be that important, or demand any of the attention that I wasn't willing to give.

I didn't realize just how awful I was to the ones closest to me until one of them refused to be my exit buddy. Whenever I brought up work, they would shut down and get quiet. I would talk about the next big thing that I was after and they would sound disinterested. I would spill out my failures, my biggest mistakes, and I would get a passive response. Of course, I didn't pick up on this as quickly as I should have… but I picked up on it eventually. I realized that as my dreams got bigger, my evil green monster would come out to play more often. I was selfish, using this person as a sounding board.

The hardest apology I've ever had to make…

And from this mistake, I learned the most important thing in life to this day. Your exit buddies are EVERYTHING. They deserve the world. They deserve a listening ear and an interested heart more than they deserve a babbling lunatic. And whether or not you continue chasing your dreams until you're ninety years old, your exit buddies deserve to come first. Before any size dream.

Find buddies who will call you on your shit, keep you accountable, and most importantly, refuse the job when you're out of control.

Those are the best ones.

#4: Roll with the punches.

This one was the hardest for me, clearly, because I was a raging loony, a naïve business owner, for years. I was in denial that I wasn't capable of rolling with the punches. I actually thought that's what I was doing.

I developed a stress twitch around year two in my business. I would blink one eye and then the other, and the more stressed I became, the more the twitch decided to come out from hiding. I looked like I was winking at everybody. And I didn't even realize just how bad it got, until a client called me out.

I was working a job out in Washington, and the twitch was out and about, as it had become the new norm. My client noticed the twitch about halfway through the day, and asked, "Is your eye okay? Do you need some contact solution? It can get really dry in here."

Trying to keep my mortified reaction at bay, I played it off as if I were totally fine. "Oh, my contact just has a little scratch on it. Thank you, though."

But then, as I tried lying (and I am incapable of pulling off a lie, so you KNOW when it's happening), I noticed my words getting softer and then completely not making sense at all. So, what's an overtired, overworked, mentally, physically, emotionally exhausted business owner to do? I told her about my stress twitch.

THANKFULLY, she was a superstar (I love that quality about women. It's as if all women have each other's backs in these matters no matter what) and we blew right past it. I finished the day better than ever, with a happy client.

A week later, I opened an envelope in the mail containing a massage gift card, a thank-you note, and a sense of grounding back to reality from an incredible woman, my kick-ass client. Everything was going to be okay. It always is, dreamers.

What I learned from that stress twitch is that stress can come in all forms and show up during various times in life as things outside of the norm of what are considered "normal" signs of stress. Those signs can be quite surprising. And as for me, I was incapable of going with the flow. I didn't know how that actually worked. Instead of rolling with the punches, I was taking them to the face. One after another.

After receiving my thank-you card in the mail, I decided to make some changes and work to become more aware of when my twitch started up. I tried to start adapting to the changes around me, the things that didn't go my way, little by little. It took quite some time, but I managed to get to a place where I could handle the little things going wrong (or differently than I expected), one baby step at a time.

Now, the twitch still comes back, but I am able to catch it the second it floats to the surface and put it back where it belongs. When I catch the twitch, I go for a walk, play with my puppy, or take the action that I have been avoiding—either in my personal life or my business.

It is possible to control how you react to the stress. The punches cannot be avoided, but you do NOT have to take them to the face.

STAYING PRESENT

Now I am going to chat about a little topic that nearly killed me. It was the root cause of having to take sleeping pills to fall asleep at night, and it stunted the growth of my business because I wasn't creating space; I was blocking it. That topic?

Staying present.

Before you go rolling your eyes because you know how to do

this, let's chat about what this actually means. Staying present in the moment means you are actually living in the now, instead of the future. As someone chasing your dream, it is way easy to get wrapped up in a week from now, a month from now, or even years from now when you want to actually arrive at your dream life (especially when you have a wall calendar for the whole year sprawled across your entire room like a birthday banner). It is easy to get stuck in the mindset of what you are working toward, instead of the life you are actually living in the now.

Staying present doesn't mean you can't think about those things, because that is inevitable and necessary. But it does mean that you cannot let those things dictate your current situation, or force your brain to be elsewhere than the present moment. Dreaming about the future and letting it ruin your present are two completely different concepts.

Allow me to let you in on a little secret. My biggest, boldest, epic ideas flow through when I allow myself to be present. These moments happen when I am in the car, doing the dishes, deep cleaning the office, or walking my dog. When I focus on the moment, I am able to not only accomplish more and perform at my absolute best, but I am able to create space for my dreams to evolve. And the best part? I am *happier*.

By constantly focusing on the future and worrying about every single detail that I would never be able to control, I was blocking the big dreams from forming at the surface. I was disabling my own success because I was worried about a future that I wouldn't even want down the road, a future that changed while I was worried about creating it perfectly.

So, the secret? Allow yourself to be right where you are. Create that space for dreams to form, and you will enjoy the journey so much more. When I was first working toward staying present, during the times when I was the most stressed, I noticed the biggest shift. Not in my business, but in my *love toward* my business. I felt free of my dream, not dependent on its success. And that's when everything changed.

LOOSEN THE GRIP

I got a grip on my stress when my world came crashing down and I had no other choice. I let my stress control my dreams and, to some extent, destroy them. I let my stress ruin the joy I had in starting toward my dream in the first place, turning that joy into resentment.

But the truth? The stress and anxiety of chasing after your dream life will always be there. And when you're chasing after the big shit, it's way easier to grip on tight and white knuckle it through life than it is to let go. But if there's one single thing that you can do for yourself to change the course of your journey in the best way possible, it is to get control over how much you allow yourself to grip. You don't have to let go completely, and I think letting go completely is not only detrimental, but impossible when your heart is in it. But you do have to release to the point where you feel like your sanity is not about to blow at any point in time.

You deserve the dream life you are chasing. And you deserve to chase it with minimal stress (notice I said minimal…we're not shooting for miracles here). It's time you took control. It's time you let go of the worry and make shit happen. The big shit.

CHAPTER 10

You Get To

Allow me to let you in on a little secret. You don't have to chase after your dreams. You don't have to do any of this. You don't have to put in the work, make the sacrifices, spend the time, energy, or sanity on going after your dream life. You don't have to.

You get to.

On this crazy, wild ride, you get a choice. You get to choose whether or not you take action. The reality of the daydreams you've spent years curating is a product of that choice.

When I was in the thick of it, I woke up most mornings

not wanting to get out of bed. I would roll over, press sleep on my alarm clock over and over again, pull the covers over my head, and refuse to move. I knew the mountain that was ahead of me, and when I creeped into the dark place, I couldn't manage to stop saying that I didn't want to. I couldn't flip it.

Most weekends, as I kissed Will goodbye before heading to the airport, I would feel this pang of anxiety as I grabbed my suitcase to walk out the door. I would almost always say to him, "I wish I didn't have to go. I really don't want to." And of course, it didn't register at the time that I was saying this about the dream that I worked so damn hard to achieve. For a good few months, every time I left the house, after waving goodbye to Will, I cried silently in the back of the cab underneath my sunglasses all the way to the airport. It was a ritual, I guess you could say.

I spent weekend after weekend, morning after morning in this state. And I got so good at it that I completely started resenting what I built. My dream company soon became the thing that I dreaded most. No amount of motivational drug could save me. I was so far gone.

That's when my anger and stress were at their peak. I felt suffocated within a company I worked so hard to create, my dream for which I sacrificed so much.

So, as a result of this gradual resentment, I began exploring other avenues of business. I started applying for jobs.

Of course, I had no idea what I wanted to do, but I craved something stable, something with no weekends, a steady paycheck, doing something I could tolerate. Communications, public relations, marketing, sales…everything. Anything.

I applied online, which was my first sign that this process was something I didn't really want in the first place. Before I started my company, I applied for every single one of my jobs in person. I would ask to speak to the manager/boss/important person in charge and hand them my resume directly as I shook their hand. I would tell them why I was a good fit for the job and *ask* for a shot at an interview. My parents taught me that, and it's worked with every single job I've ever had. When I wanted a job, I went through extreme measures to get that job. But somehow applying for these jobs online was something I couldn't quite own yet, couldn't quite grasp, and applying in person would make it real. And I didn't want it to be real. But was there another option?

I believed my love for my company had officially dwindled. I didn't think there was anything left to salvage, even though it was continuing to grow. I felt the weight and pressure and exhaustion of constantly producing sales and getting clients. I felt hurt and defeated and isolated, and I felt that no one could possibly understand.

It was paralyzing.

I didn't tell a soul. I thought that if I shared this information with anyone, I would lose all credibility. I thought that people would have a field day talking about the girl who gave up her dream company, which she scaled from scratch, to go back to the corporate world. I could imagine the disappointment from my parents, from Will, from my friends, when I told them that I was ending it (and for the record, these are people who would NEVER be disappointed in something like that). I felt the judgment that was nonexistent.

A few companies got back to me with interview requests, and I almost went to them.

Almost.

I got my wake-up bonk on the head the day before my first interview, in a big department store looking for a suit coat (I gave all of mine away to a charity when I left the corporate world). A store worker came up and asked me if I needed help with anything. I turned to her and said, "Yes, I am looking for a fitted suit coat."

As I followed her to that section of the store, all I remember is staring at the back of her head, following blindly, one foot in front of the other, shocked that my body was able to do all of this in auto-pilot. We got to the suit section, I thanked her as she walked away, and I just stared at all of the suits.

I stared until the tears in my eyes made the suit coats blurry.

I can't tell you how much time went by in that moment, but I can tell you this. The auto-pilot shut off. Something clicked. Something in my head sent an urge to my legs to walk right out of that store, without the suit coat. That same something sent an urge to my hand to dial the number of the company and cancel my interview. And that something sent an urge to my body to start the car, drive home, sit down, and GET BACK TO WORK.

I'm sure you've had moments like that, moments that you'll never be able to explain. The Universe has a funny way with pivotal moments in our lives. They never happen with these grand gestures. Instead, they happen in the suit section of a department store.

It was in that moment that I realized what I was doing to myself. The resentment, the anger, the stress. It all boiled down to flipping the script in my business. I convinced myself for so damn long that I had to keep scaling my company, as if I had no choice in the matter. I convinced myself that I *had to* do it all, slowly, yet persistently, conditioning my brain that there was not another way to live.

Well, friends, there is *always* a choice.

In the thick of it, I was so in over my head with clients, I didn't think I could say no. I was saying yes to everything because I knew I needed to in order to scale, and that yes included how I was allowing myself to view it all. I was a naïve little business owner, a business owner who just didn't know any better, tangled in the mess, so easily convinced that there was no other way.

Looking back, the time I spent looking for jobs, applying, and setting up interviews, I could have spent evaluating why

I had that urge in the first place. Because that was not just a little urge.

Guys, I could have spent that time on vacation…

Every time I hit apply and attached my resume to a job posting, I felt relief. Relief from the burden of being a business owner. It always seems easier on the other side. When you're chasing, when you're taking action, when you're up to your eyebrows in the ugly mess of it, the release button is sometimes as easy as hitting apply.

And that is the shit no one tells you.

THE DIFFERENCE
DECIDES EVERYTHING

I say this with the utmost emphasis. When you wake up and don't want to do your dream anymore, take a HARD, LONG look as to why you are feeling that way. It may not be your dream at all; it may just be the story you've told yourself as to why you have to, instead of why you get to. There is so much power in taking a step back and evaluating your mindset. And when a big idea hits—one that tries to convince you to give up on your dream life—put on a helmet, go get a manicure, and figure that shit out.

You are justified to feel overwhelmed and confused and tired and overworked and bored with your dream. That is NORMAL. But you are not justified to give it up before you've had a chance to sit down and be rational about your reasoning.

Straight up, there is nothing wrong with throwing in the towel to your dream. If you've truly fallen out of love with it, then it isn't really throwing in the towel at all. It is simply pivoting in your life to something designed even better for you.

However, if you are deciding to throw in the towel because you've slowly convinced yourself of resentment toward your dream, then you ARE throwing in the towel. You are not doing the pretty pivot. You are simply throwing a solid dream off a cliff before sifting through the reasoning behind it all.

Step back. Breathe. And put some time into your big decisions.

YOU ARE IN CHARGE OF YOUR MIND-SET

It is up to you to flip your mindset and catch yourself with the "I have to's" before they turn deadly. It is YOUR job to hold your brain accountable for the things it tries to convince you. And before you let the "I don't want to's" in, take some time to evaluate the situation. Maybe you're tired and overworked and need a break. Maybe you need a spark put back into your dream, a new idea, a new person alongside you.

Allow me to let you in to my monkey brain: "I have to wake up early to finish some work before working with a client all day… I have to stay home on a Saturday night because my week was just too crazy… I have to get to all of these emails… I have to finish these invoices before the end of the day… I have to drive three hours to a client…"

The mistake I made was allowing the "I have to's" to become permanent in my brain. They did not need to rip me apart with resentment and tear me away from the dream I worked so hard for. But I let them, one by one. I allowed my thoughts to dictate my life, and instead of being in control of those thoughts, I put the car in auto-pilot, hit the detonator, and sat back, watching the whole thing crash and burn. I made the mistake of allowing the same negative thought into my brain, over and over again: The things I "have to" do are ruining the things I "want to" do. I wasn't aware. I wasn't paying attention. I wasn't in control.

Fellow boss bad-asses, do not make the same mistake that I did. Do not let those thoughts in, and in the case that you do, do not allow them to stay. Be aware of what your thoughts are convincing you that you need.

Don't you dare let them ruin your dream.

You get to do absolutely anything in the world that you put your mind to. You get to do the big shit, the crazy shit, the 2 a.m. idea shit. You have the freedom to make it happen, every ounce of it. And you get to make it happen with a smile on your face and joy in your heart, once you make the decision to commit.

You GET TO wake up every single day and make the decision to go after your crazy ideas, and your own brain is the only thing standing in the way. You are not meant to go to a job every day that you hate. You are not meant to live a life of settling, when you know in your heart that you are made for more. It's time your dreams took back their power. It's time you commanded back the life you've always wanted. It's time you lived your days on *purpose*, and not as a reaction to the reality you've built in your head, slowly resenting things you once loved.

You are capable of insanely epic shit. It's time you took it back. It's time you made the decision to take action on what keeps you up at night.

Because you get to.

CHAPTER 11

Forgive Yourself

*T*his chapter is about grace. It is about understanding. It is about forgiving. It is about moving on.

Throughout this journey, there have been a lot of times when I've struggled to forgive myself. I've made mistakes and couldn't picture a way out, a fix, if you will.

There are a lot of mistakes that I look back on and wonder what could have been if I hadn't been so wrapped up in the thick of it. Events I could have attended, people I could have met, time I could have spent with friends and family, memories I could have made. But I will always believe that there is a reason I missed those things. There is a reason

I am here, writing this to you. Showing you that there is another way.

All those years of constant work taught me that there is so much more to life than chasing a dream. And starting out, that seemed like all there was in the world. The excitement was there, the energy, the momentum. I became obsessed, unstoppable, until reality finally hit me.

When you first decide to chase that dream, it will seem like you're alone in the Universe. Just you and your dream, having cocktails on the beach, enjoying the waves crashing and sun on your face. It will feel like the absolute most important thing at the time, and that is totally justifiable—you are trying to move a mountain, after all.

During those first weeks, months, years, you will be faced with many decisions that will require sacrifice in one way or another, whether that is sacrifice toward your dream or sacrifice toward certain loves in your life. That is just plain reality. It is something every single human is faced with constantly. Sometimes, you will make the right decision, the right sacrifice, and other times, you will feel the grip in your chest, the tears welling up.

Regardless of the decision, regardless of the aftermath, you deserve to forgive yourself, no matter what that might look like. There will be things along the way that you will cringe at the thought of and you'll want to climb under the covers and stay there for weeks. But when you are ready to face them, remember to give yourself grace, understanding, patience.

But no matter what, face them. Because if there's anything that slowly kills a person's happiness, it's the neglect to recognize what happened, process it, and make the decision to move on.

There will always be a different way of doing things. But living in a world of "what ifs" is no way to live. This is all happening for you, every choice you make, every bump in the road. It is all happening for a reason.

Will and I didn't go on dates for years. It just wasn't a thing that we did. And for the longest time, I thought that he just wasn't the romantic type, that he didn't like dates. Every weekend he would ask what I had planned, and every weekend I would tell him that I had a client booked and I was working. So, weekends would go by without an invitation to do something together. And I would feel hurt. And of course, I couldn't make plans because...work.

One night, I walked through the front door of our house, suitcase in hand, to pizza delivery on the living room table, and Will sitting there with the biggest smile on his face. I couldn't even form the words to show him my appreciation and gratitude because I was solely concerned about the client I had the next morning and how this would take away from my prep time. So, we sat there, watched a movie, ate our pepperoni and mushroom pizza, and instead of enjoying and relaxing (which was his only intention, to distract my crazy brain and give me a night off), I became more stressed because of the sleep I knew I was missing out on.

The next day, when I got home from my client, I asked him why we never go on dates. It was a subject that weighed on me for a long time, and I felt it was time we got to the bottom of it.

He said, "I would love to go on dates, but I'm not sure when we would."

Immediately, I got defensive. "There are so many times when we could…" And I stopped dead in my tracks, because I knew.

In the calmest voice, almost a whisper, he said, "No. You are always working."

I realized that the reason why we never went on dates wasn't because he didn't want to, but because I had shut him out. I had shut out our relationship. I had put everything else on the back burner, telling myself that I would find the time eventually, after the next thing.

But I never did.

We came to the conclusion that he always wanted the dates, he always wanted the experiences together, he just didn't want to make me feel bad and have to choose between him and my work.

He was being the most romantic man in the Universe, and I was failing to see it because I couldn't get out of my own damn way. He was going out of his way to make sure I had a full belly, clean sheets to sleep on, enough hugs and kisses, and a cozy house in which to come home and unwind. He was taking care of me, while waiting patiently for the craziness to subside, because he trusted that eventually it would, that we would eventually get our lives back. And without realizing it, I made him wait for a very, very long time.

People. Do NOT go years neglecting. Do NOT allow yourself to turn into a crazy work-obsessed person who cannot enjoy the simple, beautiful things in life—like mushroom and pepperoni pizza delivery and a husband who lets you eat two slices before he even asks you about your day because he knows you come home hungry as hell from a long day of work. Life is too damn short.

And when these things do happen, the neglecting, the royal screwups, as they often will when you are first starting out, learn from them, accept them as truth, and then move on… *forgive yourself*, striving to be better every single day. You deserve your fullest attention, your dream deserves your fullest attention, but so do your loved ones.

What I've found is that life is so much sweeter, so much more purposeful when you live it step by step, day by day. When you give all your energy in the present moment to the shit that you're stressed about happening a week out, well, you miss things. And somehow, life goes by faster.

Worrying about the future will eat you alive, and holding onto the stress of your past actions will even more. Let's be honest, worrying gets you nowhere except early signs of aging. And that anti-aging cream is expensive.

It's okay to make mistakes. It's okay to look back and wish you had done things differently. That is HUMAN. But it's not okay to dwell there. There comes a time when you have to make the decision to move on and move forward, learning from the mistakes.

Go through the shit, learn from the shit, move on from the shit.

I promise, if I can do this as the work-obsessed, crazy-haired monster I had become, you can too. It was one of the hardest things I've ever done, but more than worth it, and more than possible for you. You deserve a life in which you forgive yourself, a life in which you give yourself grace. And everyone else in your life deserves that forgiveness and grace from you too.

Because we're all just doing the best we can.

Raising my glass to you, boss. Yes, you can.

Onward.

CHAPTER 12

Celebrate Everything

When I first started my business and took the jump into the scary place, I bought a bunch of tiny bottles of champagne—like the ones you get on an airplane. I had this vision in my head that the first time I booked a client, the first time I hit a big goal, the first time I survived a nerve-racking phone call, I would open a tiny bottle and celebrate. I remember seeing a woman do it in a movie once, and I thought it was the coolest thing ever. And I was a business owner now, of course, so I could do these cool things like have champagne in the middle of the day in my house where I sat at my kitchen table cold-emailing potential clients. In my new business, everything was crazy exciting.

Until it wasn't.

Here's what went down.

I remember waking up one day, swamped as hell. It felt like a normal day, as this had gradually become my actual norm. That's how it happens. It's always gradual, and you come to accept the stress hives as a way of life, as if that's how it's always been.

You never realize when something changes for the worse if it happens slowly enough.

And then, there I was, a hot mess. But this time, I had no disguise. This was what I was putting out into the world. And I could actually *feel* people absorbing my energy and throwing it right back in my face.

I had emails piled up, a to-do list I didn't even want to look at, more client calls scheduled than I had time in the day, and a raw sense of urgency, not because I wanted to do all of these things and was excited for them, but because I *had* to. I was a terror when I opened my mouth (unless you were my client, because I treat them like QUEENS), and I was treating those I loved like straight garbage—because, in my world, at the time, they were not as important as my work.

Can you freaking believe that?! A little hard to process that those words just came out on paper, but I promised I would tell the whole ugly truth.

You're welcome.

Y'all, when it gets to the point when you are raging pissed at yourself because you have too much on your to-do list that you don't want to do, and you not-so-secretly hate yourself, it's time you take an uncomfortably long, hard look.

Somewhere along the line during that first year, I booked my first client, I had my first tough phone call, and I hit more big goals than I thought possible. And those tiny champagne bottles just sat on my shelf. Not once did I stop to celebrate those wins. Not once did I allow myself to take a step back and realize how far I'd come. I never stopped to celebrate the life I was creating for myself, the life I always wanted that was unfolding right in front of my eyes.

Because to me, none of it was good enough.

I was living for the next. Constantly.

Firsts are easy to recognize. The first time you book a client, the first time you finish your extra-long to-do list, the first time you see five figures in your business bank account—that is the exciting stuff; that stuff is identifiable. But the lasts? Those will knock you right over before you even get a chance to realize what is happening. Like the last time I was nice to myself, or the last meal I ate while allowing myself to feel full, or the last time that I actually had a weekend off.

The lasts don't identify themselves. The lasts are unforgiving. They just happen. And then life moves forward.

Sometimes without your consent.

The blow that hit me the hardest? The last time I enjoyed booking a client.

I can't tell you where or when the excitement faded, but eventually, it got to a point where I no longer enjoyed booking clients. I *resented* it. And the thing that was moving my dreams forward, the booking of the actual clients, stressed me out. It made me angry.

Instead of celebrating how I was creating the vision for my life and making mad progress and doing all of the things I was so damn excited to do, while building the business of my DREAMS, I turned into a living, breathing stress ball who couldn't handle her shit.

My quality of life decreased dramatically because I was so concerned about the "next big thing," and I never stopped to take in the big things as they happened in the moment.

I was very much an "if you're not moving forward, you're moving backward" person. That had been my mindset for a long time because I never knew it was an option to stand still. I never knew that stopping to smell the roses was a thing that people did. I never knew that it was socially acceptable to celebrate your wins as a business owner because I stopped putting weight into my goals.

They were transactional.

These snowballing goals—on to the next the second the goal was accomplished—were my normal until my world came crashing down, I almost lost the love of my life to the stress maniac that I had become, my mom was diagnosed, I had become absent for all of the friends in my life, I had developed an eating disorder, and my business was thriving, but I didn't actually care.

I never knew it was an option to stop until it was the only option that I had.

It was the end of year two, my life was spiraling, and I had two options: either lose everything or learn how to chill the hell out and take inventory of all of the incredible things around me. I picked the second option. After being beyond stubborn and fighting it for YEARS, it was now a life or death situation. It was a matter of my happiness, my sanity, my fulfillment, my *life*.

COMPARISON KILLS

Nothing I was accomplishing felt good enough. Because as an entrepreneur in the world of social media, nothing ever is.

Too often, we get caught in the reality of comparison of what others are celebrating. We look at other people's wins as a way to negate our own. Our win wasn't *that* big, so therefore, it is stupid to celebrate. Look at what *they* just did… We are pathetic that we are buying a celebratory sweater because of what *we* just did. Comparison is a quick way to get your ass kicked. And the person who is doing the kicking is you. Your win is justified for celebration no matter how big or small.

And I get it. Doing this whole entrepreneur thing with social media at your fingertips sometimes seems IMPOSSIBLE. How can you *not* compare yourself to the people on the Internet who are so much farther ahead than you are? How can you look at others and feel like you measure up with your baby business?

I used to really struggle with this. I would spend hours on social media looking at all of the choreographers who were posting accomplishments that were WAY bigger than mine. And by the time I got off the app, I felt like complete garbage. Worthless.

So, here's my advice when you get to that stage in the game, because you will. Get off the stupid social media. Limit your time there. Limit who you follow, who you allow to show up in your feed. When you start feeling like garbage, STOP SCROLLING, and take a hard look at why you are feeling that way.

I truly feel there is a lot that can be learned on social media when you are starting and scaling a business, but in the case that it is hindering that growth, hindering you from celebrating what is happening in *your* life, close the app. Be smarter than the phone. Don't let it win.

Cut the comparison bullshit. You are your own story, your

own success, your own life. And once you realize that, everything changes.

SCREWUPS ARE GOLD

This needs to be said, because there are very few times when we're actually told this as young business owners. It is a GOOD thing to celebrate your royal screwups. Yes, you read that right. We're not just talking about celebrating your wins, but also celebrating the times when your initial reaction was to dye your hair, eat a whole bag of peanut butter cups, and drink your weight in orange soda.

Those times are gold. They teach you everything. Your wins don't teach you shit. And to be honest, there's a solid chance that most of mine were straight luck. But for some reason, the times when I royally messed up were the times that, not long after, I saw massive success. I just had to keep pushing for a little longer to get there.

Here's the thing. So many people give their dreams the big middle finger and throw in the sweaty towel right before they are about to win. But the ones who stick it out when it gets messy and icky and really freaking hard are the ones who get where they want.

As you've learned from this book, all of my success, the success that actually mattered to me, came out of years in the depths of hell. Straight up.

You are going to make so many mistakes. You are going to

look back and say, "What the HELL was I thinking." But that's okay. That's normal. It is all a part of it. That feeling, too, shall pass. And then, after a few late nights, some curse words, and a decent latte, we're back. And suddenly, it's all good again.

THE MOMENTS

I'm a "big moments in the little moments" type of person. I believe in the impact of specific moments that change our lives. And I believe in letting that change in when it decides to enter our lives.

So, here's what happened.

It was New Year's Eve 2017 at about 10 p.m. Will and I had just finished a big dinner, celebrating, just the two of us, the year that almost killed us. We went to bed before midnight and he fell asleep almost instantly, but I couldn't close my eyes. I couldn't shut my brain off.

So, I went across the hall into my office and closed the door quietly. I sat at the desk that caused me so much anxiety during that year, in the room where I hated going. The room where I had scaled to everything, but lost just as much in the process. The room that changed everything.

I sat in that room and let myself cry.

Awhile later, I pulled out my notebook and started writing. I wrote down all of my goals for the year ahead, and I gave myself a choice. I would either accomplish those goals and thrive, or I would give up the business. I made the decision to change or move forward, not just for myself but for everyone and everything surrounding me.

I wrote down what I would need to do to keep the company, how it would need to change. Here is what I wrote...

1. Hire a team who supports you and makes your job easier, taking the tasks off your plate that cause you stress and waste stupid time that you could easily spend on the things you actually want to do.

2. Be the person you want to be. Treat your life like you've always wanted. Take it all back.

3. Attend every single social event that caused you pain to say no to in the past.

4. Stop worrying about scaling and figure out a way to start enjoying the work again.

5. Be a nice person, to yourself and to others.

6. Fix the relationships you truly care about. Now.

7. Cut the bullshit stress.

8. Get help for your eating disorder, and take control over the monster that has ruined everything.

9. Stop and smell the roses.

10. Fuck the money. Say no to what doesn't serve you, and be happy about the fact that you can.

I pulled off a piece of tape and taped these to the outside of my desk so I would have to look at them every day when I sat down to work. I looked up and something caught my eye that I always knew was there but never actually allowed myself to *see*. It was a tiny bottle of champagne. I walked over to my shelf and grabbed it. I decided it was time. Time I celebrated.

I popped it open and drank right from the bottle, smiling after every sip. Smiling about all of the epic losses and the humbling wins that, until that moment, I never actually saw as wins.

I closed my eyes in bed that night and knew that everything was about to change. The moment had come. And I was so damn excited for it. I slept for the first time in years without my sleeping pill. As I fell asleep, I cried silently, as to not wake up Will. Only this time, they were happy tears.

 I believe in the "big moments in the little moments" that change our lives. And for me, that moment in my office by myself on New Year's Eve changed it all.

You see, those first two years were enough to make me see exactly what my dream life demanded of me. They were enough to throw me over the edge and bring me back again. Those first two years changed me, they changed my mindset, and they changed my life, my future, my new normal.

I didn't need a list of tangible, step-oriented goals to get me there because I knew what I needed to do. I needed to take action. I needed to stop being a psycho asshole.

I just needed to breathe.

At the end of that following year, I sat in my office and looked at the list taped to my desk, ready to write my goals for the New Year. I pulled it off and grabbed a pen. As I read through every item on the list, I crossed each off, one by one, with so much damn pride the entire time.

Those first two years in my business taught me that EVERYTHING surrounding your dream is worth acknowledging. Worth learning from.

Worth celebrating.

PICK YOURSELF UP

I messed up. So freaking much. I made investments that I couldn't get a return on to save my life. I refused to organize my inbox and missed out on potential clients. I allowed myself to get so burned out I almost lost the love of my life, and I think I traumatized the dog past the point of no return with my constant stress. But the beauty of all of my royal fuckups is that life continued on—whether I wanted it to or not. And without them, I wouldn't be here. I wouldn't have grown. I wouldn't have made ridiculous mistakes and been able to share them with you crazy animals.

You are allowed to go down in the dumps, be pissed at yourself, perpetually turn Tuesday nights into your self-wallowing drinking parties. That is all totally okay, totally human, and sometimes, a vital step in the process. I firmly feel that if you are not getting pissed at your risky decisions and taking big jumps in your life that make you want to eat enough Chinese food to feed four grown men, then you are not doing it right. Because the beginning? Well, it's supposed to be scary. It's supposed to piss you off. Those moments are normal. And you are completely justified in going there.

But you are NOT allowed to stay there.

You pick your ass up off the ground and keep moving forward. There will be times when you are celebrating big wins, and then there will be times when you are celebrating that you brushed your hair that day. Both are worthy celebrations.

GRATITUDE

You guys, a crazy thing happens when you stop to take it all in. You start to realize that there is so much more to life than what you thought. You realize that smiling before you've had your morning coffee is a real thing that people do—not because they are crazy loonies, but because they are truly happy to be alive.

Gratitude is a funny thing. I thought it was a buzzword until I learned how to actually do it right. The thing is, gratitude can come in any form you want. You can thank the Universe for another day, smile and think of your beautiful family, and your warm house, and the food on the table, and the clean water you drink, and the clothes on your back.

Or you can do what I do.

Our tiny house in the city has leaks in the roof. Every time it rains, we listen very closely to where we hear water dripping, and then we put buckets under the spots we hear. Sometimes, we miss some spots and wake up in the middle of the night to our puppy drinking the puddle on the floor. But that's only happened a few times.

The first time we had to put buckets out, I cried. A) because I used to live a VERY dramatic life, and B) because I couldn't believe our perfect little house in the city was leaking icky rainwater all over our new house décor.

Now, when we put buckets out, I do it with so much damn joy I freak Will out. The second I hear the drip, I run to get the bucket, pick up the dog, kiss him on the forehead, and give my husband a huge hug. Because the longer I've lived this life of raw uncertainty, following my dreams and leaning into the fear, the more I've realized just how beautiful these little moments are.

These are the moments that we will remember. As long as we pay attention.

Someday, we're going to look back and tell our kids about the buckets, and listening for the drops, and slipping in the puddles the next morning. And it'll be a damn good story, because all stories that start with "Back in the day we used to…" always feel so good to tell.

So, my gratitude comes in the form of moments. It comes in the form of taking a step back to breathe it all in. And if we want to get closer to our dreams, we have to do this shit. We have to celebrate, express gratitude, even when we can't hop on board at first. Even when we have to make up our own version of the process.

Because the second it gets hard, we need something to bring us back.

GROWTH HAPPENS IN THE MESSY

Some days, you are going to get way pissed at yourself, which is the worst kind of pissed. You'll find the guilt train and hop right on board. And when the timing is just right, you'll lose your composure completely—usually on a night out in heels, or to someone you love. But nonetheless, you have to keep pushing forward. You have to force yourself to look in the mirror and get the fuck over it. To be a better human day after day.

That is where the real growth happens. It doesn't happen when you book your first client, or get the dream job, or buy the car, or finally have more than a three-figure number in your bank account. It happens when you force yourself to celebrate this messy journey, as ugly as it might seem at times, and celebrate how far you've come, who you are as a human, and this beautiful life.

So, what do I do when it gets bad and I can't seem to find a single thing to celebrate? I pick up my puppy, tell the robot in my living room to blast Christmas music, dance around the house with him—singing loudly and making up the words—make some coffee, and take a freaking breath. He loves it.

CELEBRATE ONE DAY AT A TIME

The Myth: Life should be a big party. You should be constantly laughing, constantly in awe and filled with joy. And the shit that no one tells you? The truth? Sometimes that is going to be the hardest thing in the world. Life is going to throw actual dog poop at you, and you're going to have to figure out how to clean it up and get to work on time. It is inevitable.

You need to know that it is normal to feel off. It is normal to have weeks where all motivation, inspiration, and joy are hard to come by.

Normal.

We are embarking after our dreams, people! This shit is the real deal. Along the way, there will be good, and there will be bad, and there will be very bad.

But eventually, you figure out that balance. You figure out how to go to the party, make it to bed at a reasonable hour, dodge the dog shit, and get to work early—coffee in hand.

It gets easier. You get better. You just have to be aware that there will be mistakes and major screwups.

All the more reason to celebrate.

You have to get to a place where your celebration parties for yourself and your beautiful life happen more often than the pity parties. That you are feeling the joy and radiating how you actually feel. Because if you can do that, it will happen a hell of a lot sooner. Your dreams will get closer and closer. And soon, it will be real.

This all comes from a mindset shift. A shift from the thought process of *failure*, into the thought process of *I just learned an insanely valuable lesson I couldn't have learned had I not experienced that*. And that shift is a single decision. Easy to get to, difficult to implement. But you are not most people. You can do difficult. One baby step at a time. Yes, you can.

You are to be celebrated, people are to be celebrated, this life is to be celebrated. If you are not celebrating, then you are tolerating. You are merely existing. And that is not enough. You are so much better than that.

Someday, it will all make sense. All of the failures, the big wins, and the timing of it all. But if you go years with your nose to the grindstone, well, I would call that a mistake. And take it from someone who made that mistake for too many years in a row.

There is SO much to enjoy in this life. The process of chasing your dreams is way better than the actual accomplishment of it. The process ignites something in us along the way, it teaches us what we really want, it proves what truly disappoints us, and then we prove right back that we can come out of it a better, stronger, more kick-ass human than when we started.

I lived in a space for years when I was just starting my business that makes me cringe writing about it. But I promised I would share the gory details, so, again, you're welcome.

There was one night I remember so vividly when I was working until 2 a.m. to launch my online video trainings that I had been working on for months. The site had been done for a solid week, but my loony, perfectionist self needed a week to, I don't know, tweak tiny details until I fell over and died…?!

So, the clock struck 2 a.m. and I hit the publish button on the website, made the big announcement, went live on social media, and launched my online ad. After I was done? I shut my computer and freaking went to bed. The next morning, it was just another day at the office. Nothing had changed. I was just heads down, time to get to work as soon as I woke up.

People, I worked months on that beast. I worked late hours into the night on the website, for weeks at a time. It truly was something I was proud of, looking back, but in the moment, I didn't think twice about it. It was something that I checked off the list, and then moved on to the next.

I was so heads down for five years that I couldn't even tell you the highlights and low points. It wasn't that I didn't care about them; I was just on to the next before I could even process what had happened. I wasn't celebrating. I was simply missing everything. I didn't take two seconds to pause and realize where I was and what I had done. Everything just passed on by.

Because I let it.

Guys, this shit is hard. The late nights, all the time and work for something you're not even sure is going to pay off, the frustration, the early mornings, and the fact that you care so damn much about it that when something goes wrong, it feels like someone is actually taking a knife to your chest. Yes, it is an unhealthy level of attachment. We've established that.

This shit is hard.

One more time, this shit is hard.

So, if we're not stopping to take a breath, to realize how far we've come, to celebrate the tops and the tanks, then why the hell are we doing this?

Celebrate everything.

Learn from this major mistake of mine, and I promise, you will be so much more fulfilled. You will look back and be so proud of what you've done. And along the way, you'll keep your sanity. Trust me, that is the biggest win of them all.

This whole dream-chasing thing is exciting as hell, frustrating as hell, and humbling as hell… somehow, all at the same time. Do yourself a favor, and don't live for the NEXT. Live for the NOW. Because, you brave warrior, you…this is it. This is your shot. And whether it feels like it right now or not, it is happening for you.

Wake up. Smell the roses. Feel the burn. And Keep. Moving. Forward.

CHAPTER 13

But What If

W hat if you could write an entire novel in hotel bars all across the country? What if you could do life how you actually wanted to? What if you could design your future? Buy that condo in paradise? Drive the fancy sports car that everyone judges you for, but you actually don't give a shit? Wear your favorite hoodie five days in a row, only because you work from your gorgeous house and you CAN, because you are the boss and can do whatever the hell you want.

This is all perfect in theory, but the longer you play around with the "what if," the more time you are wasting. You will NEVER get to where you want if you simply sit back and question what could be, instead of just going for it. The beauty of life is if you want it enough, you will figure out a way to get it. Period.

So therefore, after the "what if" comes a more important follow-up question, "Do I have the appropriate amount of caffeine to begin?"

I'll answer that one for you. Yes, yes, you do.

It's time you cut the shit. It's time you went for it.

Find what motivates you, take MASSIVE, CONSISTENT action, and enjoy the rough and tumble road ahead.

Your story is so unique and valuable to the world if you show up exactly as you are. My story? Girl from the city grows up wanting a specific career and working her butt off until she graduated college to set herself up for that...then took a detour into something that loudly called to her and started a company, scaling fast but losing her sanity faster... Years later, amidst the crazy stress and anxiety and harsh shit that she brought into her life, she realized that her true purpose stemmed from everything she thought was a failure, everything that made her want to quit.

You do not have to be "good" at the things you want most in life. You just have to be willing to work to get good at them. You get good at them because you fight like hell for it. Everyone has a natural gift...and the ones who work their asses off enough to see a payoff, well, their natural gift is gumption and rock-solid ambition.

The biggest detriment to society is playing life safe. Not taking the jump. Not going after what you truly want. You get one shot at this.

I say let's fucking do it right.

I feel it is my duty to share my story with the world and remind all of the beautiful souls out there chasing your dreams that it is not going to be perfect. Your story is going to be messy as hell, but it is YOUR mess. It is YOUR story. And it is YOUR epic life.

The spark inside you exists whether or not you think it does. The reason some get so caught up in questioning their purpose and calling bullshit is because they haven't yet found their spark. Maybe they've searched...or maybe they keep telling themselves, "I've looked everywhere, and I can't find it," only to find it seconds later, right under their nose.

Your purpose, your calling, is OUT THERE. It is accessible to you. You just have to reach out and grab it. And that reaching out might look like a few years of working harder than you've ever worked, doing things you never thought you would do, and taking risks. A lot of risks. But we were not given this life to waste. And the risk is more than worth the payoff.

You want to make your dreams happen? Start giving a shit. And stop walking through your life in zombie mode. Take responsibility for the things you want to see change in the world, and then go out and make it happen. The people who have made a true impact with their lives are the ones who decided to give a damn. To stand up for something bigger than themselves. And to fight like hell and work harder than they've ever worked to make that happen.

And the one thing you can do NOW that will change your life forever?

Commit.

If there's anything I hope you take from my story, it's that sometimes you have to walk through the fire to get to the beautiful ocean sunset on the other side. Sometimes you have to experiment with your life and chase after the things you think you want, because those things are what are going to lead you to what you actually want.

The beauty of this life is that the Universe has an incredible way of nudging us in the right direction. You have a dream? You have something that is keeping you up at night? You have an idea you just can't get out of your head? Commit like hell to make it a reality. Trust it. And then see where this beautiful life takes you. Stop listening to the noise, stop eating everything that is being thrown at you, and start to question what it is that is right for you. Because you are RIGHT to question everything. You get to decide what you deem as truth, and then toss out the rest. There is no reason why you should take other peoples' opinions as gold (or sometimes even your own).

Commit. To. Your. Life. "You do you" is not a cliché, trendy catchphrase, but a battle cry for those who are bold enough to take control of their own dreams and LIVE.

The real truth is that your own ideas are your future success. The moment my life started changing drastically was the moment I stopped giving a shit about what others were telling me and started listening to myself. I stopped doing what everyone else was doing. I stopped caring about them, and dove full force into what I wanted. I did the things that were different, but felt true to me. The reality is, whatever you decide to do with your life—from the clothes you wear to the people you date to the career you choose—is your own magic.

Your. Own. Magic.

The longer you're in this, the more you realize that nobody knows what the hell they are talking about. All of the people who you think have their lives together have done a damn good job at convincing you. We are all trying to figure it out. Every single day. We all hit roadblocks. We all get frustrated as hell and anxious and stressed and question EVERYTHING. But that is the human experience. And once we realize that, life gets so damn good because we can finally forgive ourselves for the off days, the imperfect days.

Get rid of the stories you are telling yourself as to what people are thinking, and why you can't do the big things. Because here's the deal, people. You have two options: You either do, or you don't. And yes, it is that fucking simple. You want to go do something really freaking cool with your life? Make the decision. Commit. And then take CRAZY action until you get to where you want. Get OBSESSED about getting there and everything that has to do with it.

And somewhere along the way, you might realize that it wasn't your dream. It was only a stepping stone to get you closer to your actual dream. But just because it isn't your dream doesn't mean it is not someone else's. And the fact that you don't want it doesn't mean it isn't a legitimate dream. It's just not YOUR dream.

So, it's time to start chasing. Dreaming. Jumping. Acting. Living. Everything you've ever wanted is waiting. And it all starts with one question.

What if?

In Closing...

I was nearing the end of a nine-hour day with a client. I was dripping with sweat, exhausted, majorly dehydrated, my hands were shaking from not eating all day, and I just wanted to go home. Creatively, I reached my cap. Physically, I could have passed out right there on the high school gymnasium floor.

As I unplugged my laptop charger while getting ready to play the music one last time, my client walked up to me with a giddy face. "Oh! We just love having you here! Since you have a few hours still until your flight, we should just go an extra hour and then you won't have to sit at the airport for so long!"

I blacked out after her last sentence.

I must have uttered something of a yes/sure/or you'll have to peel me off the floor when I'm done but why the hell not, because I ended up staying that extra hour.

I'm not sure how I made it through that hour, but I was a zombie getting through security at the airport. I was too exhausted to eat or drink, so I sat at the gate waiting for my flight, feeling like I was about to explode from the inside out. I was so angry, so resentful. I remember thinking, "This is it. I am done. I REFUSE to say yes to anything ever again.

When I get home, it's time for a glass of wine and an exit strategy meeting."

I had enough. I was done.

The beauty of these shifts in life is that they are not gentle. When you realize that you are no longer aligned to your purpose, and the vision of your dreams has changed, the Universe has a gorgeous way of jolting you into reality by pouring cold water over your head. Cold water crazy sucks at first. But then you grab a towel, dry yourself off, get some dry clothes on, warm yourself up, and fucking move forward. And you realize that if you go back to that thing, the cold-water shocks are going to continue, so you move on to the next thing, the unknown number that's been calling you for weeks, months, years, and you keep hitting the decline button. Well, embracing that shift means picking up the phone and saying, "Hello!"

I didn't give up my company after that day, but everything in me wanted to. I knew I had to get out, or figure out a way to stay in and fall back in love with it. But I didn't have a single clue how to do that.

So, as for everything else in my business, I learned how to fall back in love by taking baby steps, by learning one thing at a time. And for me, that day, I learned my cap.

I learned, through that experience and so many others before that, how to set boundaries and feel confident in my decisions to do so. Not only did I learn how to set boundaries for my clients and the people around me, but also for my work-load, the extent to which I push myself, and the amount of overwork that I allow without giving myself space and time to fill my tank.

It took a couple of months after that day to get my ducks in a row to where I felt I actually had the space to do the things I always wanted with my business, to find the love again. I flipped my mindset of "No one can do it as well as I can" and I hired a staff who supports me, motivates me, and calls me on my shit when I teeter the line of over-the-top. I started charging my worth, a number that feels good, a number that allows me to truly put my heart and soul into everything I do from the second I start working with a client all the way through to the end. I got really strict with my boundaries, with the time that I give to others before giving to myself and the ones closest to me. And I took control of my energy, which I still work toward perfecting every single day.

I went from naïve business owner to fully owning the title of Ms. Boss, Thank You Very Much. And I run a thriving business that allows me to live with freedom and joy, serving clients all over the country not just dance choreography, but also teaching them the power of empowerment and a "yes, you can" mindset. I built a community of support, a client base filled with positive role models, switching the narrative from toxic dance world to a beautiful sport I hope someday my kids decide to be a part of.

I figured out how to turn my passion into something that,

although little by little, is changing the world. And that is important. That is what every single entrepreneur should be striving for.

The thing about my story is that it's the norm for too many people chasing after a big dream with all they have. The shit never happens all at once, and that's the killer. It's the gradual changes, the one-off yeses that slowly become the norm, the seventy-hour workweeks that turn into months that turn into years, the stress that piles up and becomes depression, the feeling of obligation that eventually strips away the freedom that you're working toward, and the time spent hustling for a dream—becoming more and more engrossed in the work that you forget about the outside world and the things you once loved.

The purpose of this book is to change the narrative. To bring to light the struggle of entrepreneurs and big dreamers, and start a conversation about how we can flip the "norm" of the hustle and grind. The more we talk, the more we change. And it's about damn time.

What I've learned from the first few years in my business is that the concept of "self-made" is bullshit. Every single human who touches your life in some way is a part of the team that gets you to your dream. And the humans who remind you what's most important in life, the ones who push you to be a better person, the ones who recognize the importance of the journey and play a part in it, whether big or small, are the humans who are vital to your story.

Figuring out the "business" side of a business is not the

hardest part in starting a business. The hardest part is the emotional side, the mental side where you're dealing with all these factors that you weren't prepared for when you first started off. Because no one is talking about those factors. They're talking about "Oh, it's hard to find clients" and "Damn, it's tricky developing a structure to your day" and I'm like BULLSHIT. Those are not the hard things! The hard things are dealing with my limiting beliefs, dealing with my stress, dealing with my confidence, dealing with being "naïve and passionate" (quite possibly the best/worst combo ever), and so many other things that need to be brought to the surface. So, it's time we talked about it when we're talking about what goes into starting a business so we can bring to light the resources that can help, the support that is out there (both with starting a business and with the shit that comes after) but is completely underutilized. As an entrepreneur, as a big dreamer, as someone who has walked through the fire, I believe we need to put these topics front and center.

As a business owner, it's easy to BECOME your business. Through the good times, the stressful times, and the times when you just want to call it quits, you never realize just how much it all impacts you as a person. It's too easy to get engrossed, to go all in, and then look back and wonder how you didn't see the business mistakes barreling into your personal life.

We all have golden shit. We all have mistakes that make us better and mistakes we wish we could erase. The golden shit is what creates our story, what dictates the future. And how we respond, how we move forward, how we *learn* is how we command our dream life.

YOUR MESS IS SEXY. Your story is fucking real. Your dreams are going to change the world. It might take a little while, it might get ugly, and it might involve some vodka-smelling Wednesday mornings...but it WILL happen if you commit. The decision is yours. And ONLY yours.

We are not in this to please others. Our voices are too big. Too powerful. Too capable. The only thing that matters is our connection to our purpose...to the dreams that keep us up at night, or daydreaming in the office...the dreams that are scary because they actually MEAN SOMETHING to us.

So, wherever you are in the process, embrace the hell out of it. Know that you are drawn to your dreams for a reason. And although that reason might not be crystal clear right now, you just have to keep putting one foot in front of the other. One step at a time. One moment at a time. And eventually, it becomes clear.

Chasing your dreams is NOT meant to be easy. The Universe does a phenomenal job at testing you to see just how badly you want what you say you want. So, go and fucking prove it. Put in the late nights and the early mornings, the work that feels uncomfortable and weird and funky, the time that you don't want to be working, but know you have to. Because it is bringing you one step closer to the life you've made up in your dreams.

The beauty of your time here is that you are the only one who decides the actions that you are going to take, the volume of those actions, and the determination to rise, despite the total failure of some of those actions. You hold unbelievable authority over your dreams, and you are only capable of doing what you *allow* yourself to do.

And all of the shit that you walk through on the way is for a reason.

It is golden.

You are meant to LIVE this beautiful life. You are meant to THRIVE. You are meant to take the scary leaps that bring you closer to your power. The "dream life" is not a buzz phrase. It is REAL. And every single step you take toward it will give you insane clarity. Sometimes, the dream life you thought you wanted is really just a lesson—catapulting you into the direction you are truly meant to go.

When I first started the shift and decided I was going to share my story with the world, I wrote this in my notes to look at periodically. It made me realize just how much of a fucking blessing this life is. This is my "why" statement. Still true to this day. The reason I did it all. Stuck through the mess, the anxiety, the stress, the depression, and the total self do-over. The reason I found my north again.

You are going to write a bestselling book that kickstarts your career as a writer. Then, you are going to speak on stages all over the world and empower millions of people, coming home to your beautiful life—your incredible husband, Will, long walks on Saturday morning, your dream house with the balcony in the bedroom and the gorgeous office and the ability to travel to your condo on the ocean whenever you want. You are going to make enough in that first year to set up your parents for a beautiful retirement and make sure your siblings are taken care of. And you are going to do all of this over and over again, with joy in your heart and alignment in your soul.

This is the reason I continued to get out of bed every day when it was hard. On the days when I could barely breathe. This whole process brought me to the dark place, more often than I would like to admit. At times, it made me feel small and worthless and insignificant. But THIS is why I came back. This is why I continued to push toward my dreams.

It doesn't have to be like this. It doesn't have to destroy you. Which is why I have made it my life goal to get my story out to the masses. To impact the dreamers...and spark action in the doers.

Don't EVER let some person or some experience make you feel small. And if you ever do feel small, take a hard look in the mirror at what is making you feel that way, because it will ALWAYS be, without a doubt, your own thoughts. Control your thoughts, control your life. Just because someone thinks you are a fraud who will never amount to anything does not mean it is true. Unless you make it so.

Your journey will be crazy. You will encounter things along the way that will make you lose your faith in humanity altogether—the weird shit. But a shower, a hot latte, and some good '90s feel-good music, and life will snap you right back. There is no "right" way. The right way is YOUR way. Period. So, before you lose faith, before you throw in the sweaty, gross, wet towel, remember why you started. Remember your "why."

If there is one single thing I hope you take from this book, it is this: You are beyond fucking capable.

Your dreams will not look the way you once thought, and that is a GOOD thing. Your story will be messy and crazy and leave you a little scuffed up and bruised, but still epic and beautiful. And the more you embrace this—the more you OWN your dreams, own your life, and own your story—the more you realize just how radiant this whole life thing is.

What no one tells you is that going through the shit is necessary and inevitable, and in order to move forward, you have to figure out how to get through to the other side ON YOUR OWN. I guarantee your shit will look nothing like my shit. And trust me, you don't want it to. But you will also never get a step-by-step manual to guide you through getting out of it.

Throughout the process, I was embarrassed that all of this shit was happening. I couldn't wrap my head around the fact that I was making so many mistakes, doing so many things that were flat-out wrong. I was a clueless little bunny hopping around from one mistake to the next, unsure if I would ever be able to spend a Wednesday morning without feeling nauseated. I kept thinking, *Is this really normal? Do people actually go through this shit?! This can't be right… Maybe this whole chasing my dream/starting a business thing isn't for me, because clearly, I SUCK AT IT!*

My dear, sweet friends, I have come to find that these are normal thoughts. You will not have a clue when you are first starting out, and that is kind of a good thing. I was naïve to everything falling apart around me because I was so wrapped up in my passion for the work. Which, looking back, was a blessing because I would have quit. I would have stopped right then and there, given up on my dream, and gotten the hell out of that madness. I would have killed my own momentum just before I made it to the level of success I had always dreamed of, but never actually thought possible.

I want you to learn from my shit and apply it to your own. I want you to know that it is possible to go through the shit AND have your dream life. It is possible to do the hard things and still have a dream that you love, a goal that you are working toward, a future that you don't resent. It took me awhile to discover this, but the shit is beyond necessary. You just have to stick it out. And this is when I tell you that you CAN stick it out. Don't you dare try to tell me otherwise.

Walking through to your dream despite the mistakes is still possible. Yes, it feels uncomfortable as hell, but it is necessary, it is normal. It is human.

My mistake was thinking that I was going to be comfortable throughout the process, but little did I know, I felt comfortable about 3 percent of the time during those first few years of my business. Most of the time, I was flailing.

The shit no one tells you.

But here's the secret… That feeling never really goes away; you just get damn good at dealing with it. Eventually, it doesn't faze you, and that is when the awesome, epic dreams come true.

Me? I hired a team. A group of people supporting me, working toward my dream together. And throughout working with them, I was able to help them realize their big dreams too. I took a step back in my company and chose my mental health over absolutely everything else. And with taking a step back, I fell in love with it again. That initial spark that I felt in the beginning is stronger than it ever was when I first started.

I realize now, it all happened for a reason. It didn't happen to me. It happened for me.

I don't want you to be scared off by this book. I want you to be prepared. I want you to know that it is crucial to feel uncomfortable—that means you are taking risks and doing the hard things. I want you to know that there will be times that will royally suck, but there will also be times when you go running out your front door, down the block, bringing it back around, and doing twenty jumping jacks before heading back inside, because you're that fucking excited.

Too many people don't go after their dreams because they want to avoid the icky feeling. Because that feeling is HARD, and most people don't make it past that. But you... you are not most people. You are capable of feeling the fear, feeling the icky, the uncomfortable, the bumpy, and pushing through despite it. You are capable of doing the hard things, because now you are prepared.

Now you know.

It's time to take on your dream, head first. It's time to embrace the shit that is to come and start moving forward. You got this, boss.

May your coffee be strong, your dreams stronger, and your energy fucking unstoppable.

Acknowledgements

Ok so, wow. I owe this book to so many people who helped make it all possible.

Will, I stopped keeping track of how many different times I wrote the thoughts I have for you in this section. I finally realized that words could never be enough. I love you.

Mom, thank you for the endless edits, mornings with Starbucks and sticky notes, and for helping me realize that this was my dream all along. You are the reason I go after the big things with passion and resilience. You have taught me how to truly live.

Dad, thank you for showing me what true fearlessness looks like. I know how to protect my dreams and defend the loves most important to me, and I will spend the rest of my life owing that all to you.

Ron, Ash and Mike, thank you for supporting all the madness, calling me on my shit when things got sticky, and being the siblings the world only dreams about from movies and books. I got damn lucky.

Reba, thank you for your incredibly detailed work copyediting this book.

ACKNOWLEDGEMENTS

And to Dana and the team at Outskirts Press, I am forever grateful. You made this dream a reality, and I couldn't have done it without you.

CPSIA information can be obtained
at www.ICGtesting.com
Printed in the USA
LVHW090055080820
662304LV00005B/733

9 781977 226419